Joel Shapiro

Tracing the Figure

Des Moines Art Center

This first edition of

Joel Shapiro: Tracing the Figure

is limited to four thousand copies
contents copyright Des Moines Art Center 1990
Library of Congress catalogue number 90-081832
ISBN 1-879003-00-7

This catalogue is published on the
occasion of the exhibition
Joel Shapiro: Tracing the Figure
organized by the Des Moines Art Center.

Exhibition curated by Julia Brown Turrell
Catalogue designed by Annabel Wimer
Printed by Holm Graphic Services, Inc.

Exhibition:
Baltimore Museum of Art
Baltimore, Maryland
21 August – 7 October, 1990

Des Moines Art Center
Des Moines, Iowa
17 November, 1990 – 13 January, 1991

Center for the Fine Arts
Miami, Florida
6 April – 2 June, 1991

Acknowledgements

Julia Brown Turrell, Director

It is our great pleasure to organize this exhibition and catalogue of Joel Shapiro's sculpture; we were particularly interested in focusing on the figure in Joel Shapiro's work, following this image and subject from the early seventies to the present.

In this exhibition, one can trace an extraordinary investigation into the complex nature of abstraction and figuration and the representation of the human figure in the work of one of America's foremost contemporary sculptors. Through this work of Joel Shapiro, one can also study issues of abstraction and figuration in a pivotal moment in the evolution of sculpture and a key point in contemporary art history: moving away from the Minimal self-referential object and into the re-inclusion of the figure, movement, and emotion.

It has been a pleasure to develop this exhibition and its catalogue with Joel Shapiro and I thank him for his generous engagement in, and support of, this project. His dealer, Paula Cooper, has been wonderfully supportive and helpful through the course of this project. I thank her as well as members of her staff, Cass Stachelberg and Natasha E. K. Sigmund. The artist would particularly like to thank Lindsay Walt for her assistance in the organization of the exhibition and his wife Ellen Phelan, for her invaluable assistance and advice in all stages of the exhibition and its catalogue.

The entire staff of the Art Center is to be thanked for all they do to realize the programs of the Art Center. I want to thank, in particular, Deborah Leveton, Associate Curator, for her assistance in the organization of this project and for the insightful interview she conducted with the artist; Margaret Willard, Registrar, for her care in arranging for packing and shipping of the exhibition; Wayne Masterson, Chief Preparator, for his thoughtful work with the artist in designing the installation of the exhibition at Des Moines; and M. Jessica Rowe, Associate Director, for all her assistance on this project. Former Associate Curator, Cornelia Butler, currently Curator of Artists Space in New York, was an invaluable partner in the early stages of this project. Annabel Wimer has been a very special participant in this project through designing the catalogue. We thank her for her creativity and all her good work.

We are very appreciative of the partnership of the Baltimore Museum of Art and the Miami Center for the Fine Arts for participating in the tour of this exhibition and allowing this body of work to be seen by a larger audience. I particularly thank Arnold Lehman, Director and Brenda Richardson, Deputy Director for Art (and) Curator, Painting and Sculpture of the Baltimore Museum of Art and Mark Ormand, Interim Director and Curator of Exhibitions of the Miami Center for the Fine Arts.

We are grateful to the National Endowment for the Arts, for their partial support of this exhibition and its catalogue and we extend a very special thanks to the Anna K. Meredith Trust for their generous support of this exhibition. The Anna K. Meredith Trust has been a major supporter of the Art Center for many years and its generous support has made possible the development and realization of numerous exhibitions, catalogues, and educational programs, as well as providing crucial and fundamental operating support to the Art Center. We are most grateful to Anna K. Meredith for her original insight and far reaching generosity and to the thoughtful support of the board of the Anna K. Meredith Trust and its Chairwoman, Mell Meredith Frazier. We are most grateful to the Board of Trustees of the Des Moines Art Center for their ongoing support of this institution and all its programs.

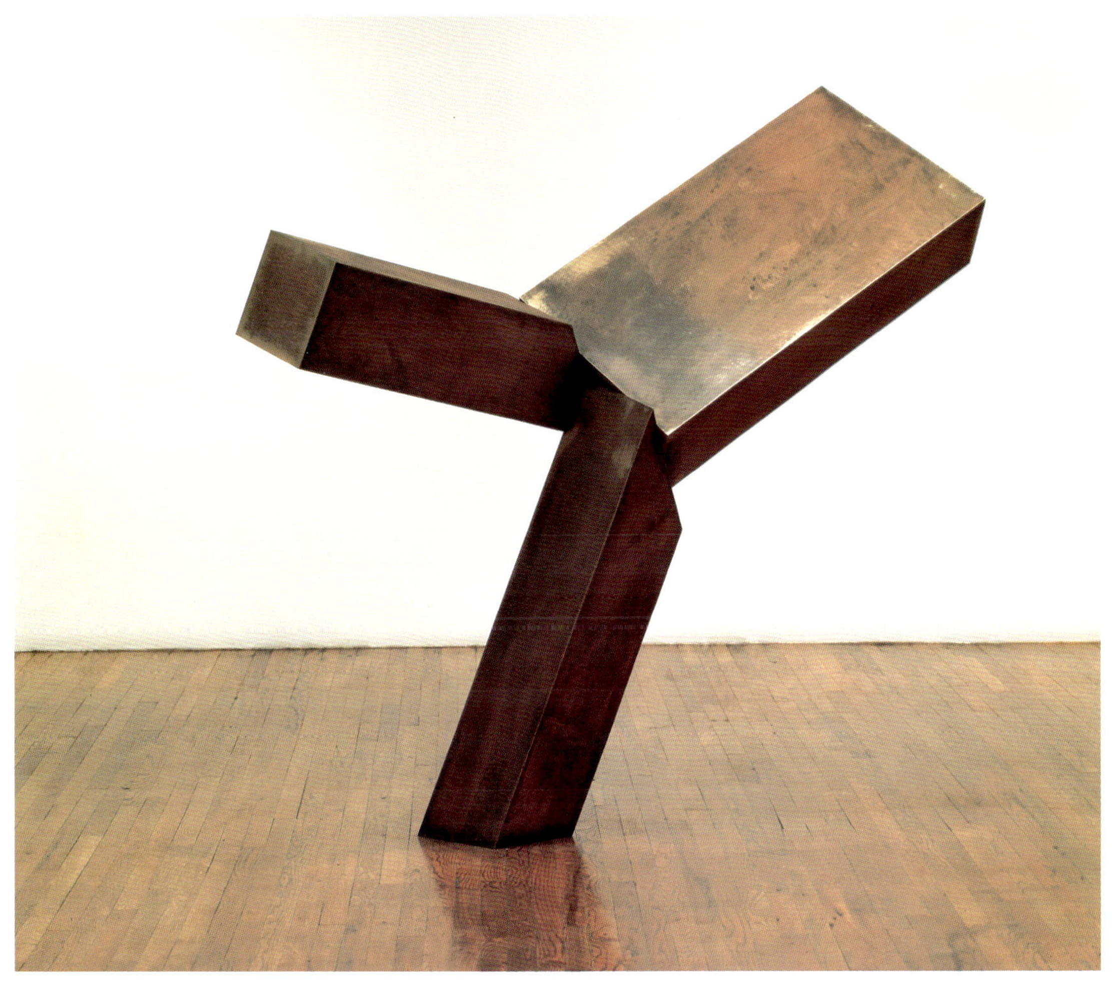

Plate 1   Untitled, 1989 (JS 866)

The Aliveness of Tentative Form: Joel Shapiro's Sculptures

Donald Kuspit

To call Joel Shapiro's sculptures "Minimalist" is to miss their point: they do not have the blank, affectless look of pioneering Minimalist works — the sense of emptiness chewing its cud. Yes, there is the return to geometrical basics — "fundamentalism" — associated with Minimalism. But there is nothing of the facile certainty of the gestalt in his art — no idolization (however tongue-in-cheek) of axiomatic form, whether implied or self-evident. Shapiro's sculptures do not have the aclimatic negative presence,[1] the entropic vacuousness, the defiantly mute and static literalness, the expressivity — cancelling seriality, typical of Minimalist sculpture. His sculptural object does not have the simplistic isolation and apartness of the Minimalist object: the avoidance of involvement that is a ritualization — the very dregs — of the Modernist idea of the "self-referential," autonomous art object. Shapiro's sculptures do not play the old guess-my-identity game: am I an ordinary object or an art object? (The predictably paradoxical answer is, of course, both.) They do not toy with the conventions of obviousness, manipulating them so as to achieve a look of trivial unfamiliarity, as though that was the whole point of the art "revision." They are not about unbanalizing banally self-evident form. Shapiro's sculptures have a more complex identity than Minimalist sculpture; their physicality is subsumed in physiognomic purpose, rather than a simplistic spatial physiology. Nor do they deliberately eschew cultural associations, as Minimalist sculpture does; but neither are they "literary," that is, they do not evoke and elaborate foretold meanings, twicetold messages, making them seem less predictable than they are. They do not invite us to recollect in aesthetic tranquility a story we already know, imaginatively defer through the delay of art experiences we have already mastered, and that before we even had them were mediated and mastered in social myth.

Instead, Shapiro's sculptures are intensely alive — uncannily motile. Even when a Shapiro sculpture is compact and self-contained, it conveys a sense of irksome flexibility — of a quasi-figure struggling towards spontaneity, but for some reason inhibited in its efforts. The result is a kind of jerky, sometimes even explosive, motion, which is formalized into fixity. Movement is made spatially precise, however illusory the precision. The "as if" figure becomes a kind of exclamation point, dynamic in itself but static in space. It may seem strange to say so, but Shapiro's sculpture belongs in the tradition, dating at least to the beginning of this century, of rendering the figure in rapid motion, as an indication of its modernity. But where, since Futurism, the effort has been to dissolve the figure's matter into motion so that only the motion is evident — the representation of motion, not matter or for that matter the figure, being the real issue, indeed, motion being more real than matter, subsuming it, and in the end being supposedly true reality — in Shapiro's case the figure's body remains solidly, even vividly (texturally) given. Moreover, where past modernist efforts to convey motion pretended to an objectivity and scientificness they did not have — artists seemed to assume that art could "analyze" in detail what is inherently difficult to render — Shapiro's sculptural bodies have an uncanny subjective inflection. They are only nominally observed beings: their dynamics has an expressive rather than descriptive point. It is less the result of the modernist use of pure movement to make a conceptual point about the mechanistic dismantling and depersonalization of the human in the modern period, than of the antithetical modernist ambition: recognition of the inherent "movingness" or expressivity of form, its cryptic personalization. Shapiro's "as if" figures reconcile the conceptual and expressionistic senses of dynamic movement, or at least exist on the borderline between their contradictory meanings, if finally, in my opinion, tilting towards the expressionistic. His sculptures move in an erratic, forceful way, rather than in a smooth synchronous one, as is typical from Edward Muybridge's photographic studies of figures in motion to Naum Gabo's "moving" spatial constructions. (Such slick coordination of parts invariably appears facile because it does not acknowledge the apparent metamorphosis of form effected by motion.) Indeed, the apparently chance character of the placement of parts in a typical Shapiro sculpture is not unreminiscent of that in an Arp concretion, for all the morphological differences between them.

Shapiro's sculptures are unbound in form, even when they are volumetrically dense. Through this unboundedness or openness of form, they generate strong affect, however ambivalent. The sense that a Shapiro sculpture is unrestrained — refuses constraint, even defying an invisible boundary, willfully breaking an implicit frame — and thus open to and unpredictably involved with surrounding space, is as crucial to the sculpture's identity as the sense of it as articulating a particular motion. In fact, the sculpture's look of intense motion is in large part derived from its lack of closure. The body of a typical Shapiro sculpture is a structure of contradictory directions — jutting parts at odd angles to each other, insecurely tied together however subtly attuned to one another. The incoherent, precarious, asymmetrical structure seems to concentrate and radiate energy simultaneously. Each limb — and a Shapiro sculpture is in effect all limbs — seems to be an awkward crystallization of energy, but also its blind discharge. Shapiro achieves a tenuous balance of forces, as well as of forms.

It must be emphasized that the uncanny sense of affect evoked by Shapiro's peculiar "bodies" — sometimes looking like deadweight, at other times airily lightweight; sometimes like a geometrical monumentalization of the figure, at other times like a deflationary attenuation of it — is not aroused through associations, but through sheer complication of form.

Unfortunately, many of Shapiro's works have been all too readily identified as figures or other familiar objects, such as houses and chairs, as though they were nothing but abstractions from these intimate realities. The imagistic character of many of the works encourages this belief, as evidenced in certain untitled works that have come to be commonly described as Untitled (Maquette for Coffin), 1971 and Untitled (Chair), 1974, among other works. The memory of a familiar object — or rather, as I believe, what can be called the image of an object, its primordial affective form — is indeed involved in a Shapiro sculpture, but it also exists in and through a strictly formal act. That is, it is as though, in putting together the objective elements of each sculpture in search of a formally valid structure, he realized he had created a strangely evocative figure. What began as a mechanical construction becomes a quasi-organic creation — a mysterious figure. The disparate interpretations of a Shapiro sculpture converge in the conception of it as a screen memory, that is, the condensation of many psycho-formal experiences of something really given in one emotionally pregnant, deep, half-fantastic memory. (As I conceive it, a screen memory is a compromise form, in which the actual experience of the formally literal object and the sense of its imago converge. Any memory can be regarded as a compromise between an experience of an actual object and an intuitive recognition of its sedimented image. This is why a memory seems "duplicitously" charged — simultaneously evoking an experience of an object and approximating to an absolute idea of it.)

But the important thing about a Shapiro sculpture is that its memorable, affective quality, even the general sense of its character as a primordial screen memory, is a consequence of the peculiar uncertainty and tentativeness of its form — the sense that it is an abstract construction deliberately embodying and structuring, as it were, tentativeness and uncertainty. (Such an understanding once and for all lays to rest the notion of it as essentially mechanistic in import.) This is why a Shapiro sculpture seems disoriented in itself as well as disorienting in space, why it seems unplaceable rather than fitting into place. It seems to fit nowhere, and to be "unfit" in itself. This general aura of "unfittingness" is crucial for the interpretation of its affect.

A Shapiro sculpture evokes a sense of dislocation partly because it rarely fits into horizontal and vertical coordinates with ease — rarely con-forms to them. It seems to defy the neutral universality and seeming inevitability of the grid, struggling with it as though it was an imposition. Certainly its terms do not seem adequate to the sculpture, in contrast to Minimalist sculpture, which fits comfortably in the grid. Even when a Shapiro sculpture seems to reduce to the vertical or horizontal, as in an untitled, unequivocally vertical work of 1987-88 (JS 793, Pl. 24), its manne-quin-like body is sufficiently amorphous to contradict, as it were, the sense of regularity and or-der — constancy and clarity — of space the coordinates imply. In general, the unresolved structure of Shapiro's sculptures — some of them unresolved almost to the point of unruliness — is of their essence, and as such at the center of their meaning. Their irresolution is an end in itself, rather than an indicator of irony and paradox. It generates the apparently open, indeterminate expressive effect of Shapiro's sculptures — but many of them can be read as absolutized anxiety, not simply as generally emotional — and their unexpected "philosophical" import. Because they refuse Cartesian space, as it were, they seem to restore, in a kind of "medieval" way, occult significance and affect to space. That is, they irrationalize space, the way perspective once rationalized it.

Uncertainty is ambiguous in import; the enemy of life, a source of anxiety, it is at the same time a stimulus to the playful reconceptualization of it. John Dewey has written that "the quest for certainty is a quest for a peace which is assured, an object which is unqualified by risk and the shadow of fear which action casts. For it is not uncertainty per se which men dislike, but the fact that uncertainty involves us in peril of evils. Uncertainty that affected only the detail of consequences to be experienced provided they had a warrant of being enjoyable would have no sting. It would bring the zest of adventure and the spice of variety."[2] For Dewey, uncertainty can be a worthwhile risk, as in experiments uncovering new aspects of reality, in effect affording fresh experience of it. Such experiments are a kind of play with reality, all the freer when they involve a loosening of control, if not threatening complete loss of control. Shapiro's sculptures can be regarded as kinds of experiments. They involve taking unaccustomed risks with seemingly familiar objects — reconstructing them so that they seem on the verge of disintegration, yet are in effect reconceived as uncanny forms. One has only to recall the modernist conception of art as a kind of "experiment" with reality — a kind of "research" into it — to realize how deeply rooted in modernist ideology Shapiro's sculpture is.

Despite Picasso's belief that "to find, is the thing" not "to search," and his objection to the notion of cubism as "an experiment which is to bring ulterior results" — to articulate "philosophic absolutisms" rather than to deal "primarily with forms, and when a form is realized it is there to live its own life"[3] — the fact of the matter is that modernism is essentially experimental, not for any ulterior philosophical motive, but in creative response to reality. Modernist experimentalism springs from the modern recognition that reality is not as immutable and resolved as had traditionally been thought. More deeply, it springs from the recognition that, as Dewey wrote, the very effort to establish formal certainty about reality betrays its basic character as process, and leads to a rigid — rather than flexible and creative — relationship to it. Experimentalism is simultaneously a means of acknowledging and of participating in the process of reality, as it is realized through a flexible, creative — "experimental" — relationship with it.

Thus, experimentation with form is a kind of intuitive re-searching of reality. Its case is re-opened, as it were. The idea that the artistically re-realized or re-found form of reality lives its own life — re-envisioned and re-articulated as in process, rather than as final and closed — implicitly acknowledges that the form represents, in however cabalistic a way, a vital new relationship to, and insight into, reality. Shapiro's sculpture as a whole — particularly certain highly eccentric works — is an experiment in pure form that suggests a certain idea about and implies a certain relationship to real form. His sculpture in effect metamorphoses real form into pure form, suggesting not only the deceptively autonomous reality of pure form, but the inherently "experimental" character of real form. More exactly, his sculpture is an artistic act of "re-forming" that implies a re-experiencing of reality, involving an indirect disclosure of its hidden emotional sense to the artist — at its best a universal emotional sense. Shapiro's sculpture communicates the "Eureka" excitement of discovery, more particularly, that special excitement that comes of realizing that what one thought one had gratuitously — playfully, "experimentally," freely (with as few preconceptions as possible) — invented is in fact a discovery of something profoundly real. It is the excitement of realizing that pure formal invention is a profound reconceptualization — re-cognition — of real objects, and thus that it has more than stylistic significance. Such formal invention has the aura of revelation, because it was arrived at intuitively and seems to articulate a fundamental truth.

Thus, Shapiro's sculptures articulate "potential space," as it has been called: they exist transitionally in an "intermediate area . . . between primary creativity and objective perception based on reality-testing."[4] This transitional area is a zone of formal experiment. Shapiro's sculptures are a kind of transitional object: they are overt experiments in form that signify covert experiments in feeling, reflective of the new sense one has of one's self when it is face to face with new reality — the unknown space beyond oneself. The unconscious ambition of such experiment has always been to create the illusion that the form invented by one's creative subjectivity somehow — secretly — corresponds to a perceivable, analyzable external reality. Form experienced as convincingly or genuinely experimental — in the conventional sense of "experimental" — is radically subjective in origin and import, even if the subjectivity that gives the form its momentum and shape — "momentous" shape — is difficult to describe. Indeed, it must seem too complex to articulate verbally to seem authentic. It must seem to exist ineffably — strongly felt but without words to "sustain" it, indeed, without even the necessity for words. Pure visual form must seem to be simultaneously prior to and beyond them, that is, peculiarly pre-verbal and post-verbal, suggesting that language is an interlude beside the ultimate point of reality. Shapiro's sculptures achieve this kind of radiantly subjective form that yet seems to signify a recognizable object, if recognizable only in and through memory — where language also seems to fail, or at least falter.

Truly experimental art, such as Shapiro's, transcends the existing language of form, in implicit acknowledgement of the fact that language "is incapable . . . of expresing the most cherished and deepest thoughts," that the "most personal thought is speechless, subterranean, unconscious, and the struggle of the creative forces with mute nature," and that "inner muteness is the real human personality."[5] For an artist to defy the accepted language of form to which he or she is expected to comply is for him or her to attempt to articulate this inner muteness, in an appeal, as it were, to the deepest subjective-creative power. (Often, a good part of the emotional energy and intellectual effort of artistic experiment is devoted to undermining the seemingly innate tendency to comply — to undoing the artist's inner expectation that he or she ought to "conform," inhibiting creativity. Not infrequently, seeming "authentic" form is generated simply out of such inner conflict, that is, out of opposition to generally acceptable, known forms.)

The effort is always peculiarly futile and ironical, because if the artist becomes successfully "non-con-formist," his or her experimental forms are culturally appropriated as a new stylistic language. The psychosocially radical point of his or her oppositional ambition is ignored, even dismissed as self-deception. Presumably he or she simply wanted to be freshly inventive. In any case, Shapiro, without being calculatedly non-conform-ist, succeeds in generating some sense of the inner muteness of human being, and of the creative struggle with the muteness of things. His work compounds these apparently antithetical mutenesses, or rather, suggests their correlation. The best of his sculptures imply that the muteness of human being and the muteness of being as such — "formally" being — are the same. The air of absolute muteness in Shapiro's sculptures is overpowering, especially because the sculptures are so dynamic — so expressively beside themselves that they disintegrate into part-objects. It is just because the best of Shapiro's sculptures seem so overtly tentative and expressively forceful, that their muteness is all the more resonant.

Shapiro's sculptures are typically small and intimate, but not exactly geared to human scale. They seem more or less — often more — out of human reach. They take the human figure as their point of departure — and ultimate return — but they trans-form it into an other-than-human, if still subliminally human, presence. If one thinks in terms of the categories of Gaston Bachelard's *Poetics of Space* — all of which implicitly take the standing figure as the measure of space — none seem applicable. At best, the categories of the miniature and of intimate immensity seem to work, as does, in a limited way, the dialectic of inside and outside, for a few sculptures.[6] In Shapiro miniaturization, intimate immensity, and the dialectic of inside and outside, exist not as goals in their own right, but for their uncanny effect. That is, they are the means by which an external representation of the self and its attributes or signifiers are converted into an internal representation. For each of these strategies of spatial articulation creates a discrepant object, as it were: something banally known becomes unexpectedly strange, and thus implicitly unpredictable in effect, more precisely, evoking unexpected, even unnamable, feelings. What looks matter-of-fact at first glance is in fact all too small; what seemed a trivial part of the world is suddenly disclosed as a mysterious world in its own right; what seemed to be solid through and through is suddenly revealed to be insubstantial, hollow. Shapiro uses these strategies to destroy our sense of what is intuitively right. Commonplace objects — indeed, the human figure, that most commonplace of objects — are experienced as expressively uncommon by reason of Shapiro's spatial manipulations. They become emotionally "impossible." In the very act of "objectifying" the figure — articulating it as a concatenation of forms, in as if Cubist Style, equivocally Analytic and Synthetic — Shapiro gives it an unspecifiable subjective aura. It is important that it be experienced as expressively special, but even more important that we be unable to concretely state the character of its expressivity. This enigmatic effect is crucial, for it is what convinces us that the sculpture's experiment in form does indeed represent an experiment in feeling. Thus, Shapiro's sculptures create a new depth of expressive implication. He realizes, with genuinely spare eloquence, the expressive potential implicit in Cubism from its first spatial disruptions — its first articulation of the tentativeness of space, ultimately its use of disruption to convey the innocent uncertainty of the body's relationship to itself. He has found a new way of making the implicitly experimental character of the self's existence explicit.

In an untitled 1987 work (JS 767, Pl. 22) what can be taken as the formal analogue of a striding figure is in fact a grouping of four slightly off shapes, two at right angles to each other and the other two balanced precariously on top of these "legs." What counts for me as much — indeed, ultimately more — than the difficult, but workable, balance are the even more difficult edges that quirkly appear at the joints. These very visible, altogether untoward edges appear because the parts, while generally conforming to the "idea" of a figure, are loosely placed. They do not neatly come together; indeed, Shapiro is entirely against such technical "perfection," for it would undermine the sense of experimental tentativeness essential to the sculpture. Moreover, the edginess of the work — as much a part of it as its volumes — makes clear that the figural construction is not a mannequin, a workable puppet on invisible strings. It undermines the figural import conveyed by the general configuration, returning us to the sense of the sculpture as an "arbitrary" experiment in form — feeling, indeed, a seemingly "direct" transcription of feeling into form, for feeling always seems "on edge" and "at the edge," being transitional to other feelings. One might say that Shapiro's "off" edges are simply another factor in the stylized awkwardness of his figures, if it was not the case that his awkward edges make their brokenness unequivocally clear. They are objective correlatives or formal transcriptions, as it were, of the internal representation of the narcissistically injured self, fragmented in such a way that it can never again be integral. Its parts no longer fit together; they are no longer adapted to one another, although they strain to be — formally. This maladaptation is ultimately what the odd edge at almost every odd angle signifies. The emotional oddness of the awkwardly put together figure seems to me particularly poignant in JS 497, (Pl. 10), which can barely put one step in front of another.

Shapiro gives us a figure standing on its head (JS 467, Pl. 9), figures on their backs (JS 155, Pl. 3 and JS 735, Pl. 20), another crouching (JS 593, Pl. 13), another militantly striding (JS 167A, Pl. 4), another leaping like a dancer (JS 909, Pl. 26), and another laying on its side (JS 466, Pl. 8). Such figures as JS 383A (Pl. 6) and JS 793 (Pl. 24) seem female rather than anonymous or male. Others seem coyly and even humorously figural, such as JS 465 (Pl. 7); JS 584 (Pl. 11); JS 712 (Pl. 18); JS 624 (Pl. 16); JS 612 (Pl. 15); and JS 766 (Pl. 21). Shapiro seems to escape a figural reading in JS 720 (Pl. 19) and JS 790 (Pl. 23), in effect groupings of thick and thin elements, and JS 587 (Pl. 12), a kind of wedge. But they seem perversely figural; the opening in the latter suggests an orifice, and the former scrambles figural parts to construct a "surreal" figure, not unrelated to some of Picasso's figural constructions. No doubt I am overstating — forcing — the figural implications of Shapiro's sculptures. But I am trying to make clear that, if not directly figural, they are haunted by the idea of the figure. However few or many parts to a Shapiro sculpture — three and four are standard, although there are five-and six-part works — its basic economy of means is inseparable from its articulation of what is emotionally basic about the lived body.

Not only is Shapiro conveying his interior sense of himself, but he is working through his object relations, to use psychoanalytic parlance, in effect "clarifying" his attitude to those who in-form his psyche. Indeed, to inhabit the limbo of pure form — and especially to magically bring a purely formal construction to haunting figural life — suggests a kind of regression in the service of ego control: Shapiro has in effect refined the emotionally disturbing relationships of the remote past into the gold of purely formal relations in the eternal present of the work of art. He reverses the scale of events: figures that were once big in his life have been reduced in size, even as they remain uneasily significant. Sometimes his sculptures seem stubbornly given, even truculently epic, and other times whimsical, almost lyric. In either case, the sculpture is more of an event than an object. Shapiro's sense of vulnerability to the original figures in his life is "internalized" in the formal sculpture: vulnerability persists in stylized, even ritualized unstableness. That has been purified — brought under control — as much as the intimate bodies of the remembered objects. Instability is particularly climatic and memorable in JS 595 (Pl. 14). Precariously balanced on one leg, with all four limbs flying off in opposite directions, the tense, uncertain relations between its parts — its internal structure — symbolizes tense, uncertain relations with primary objects, still strong presences despite their distant abstract character. Shapiro's sculptures, then, are ambiguously figural and pure — esoterically figural and exotically pure. It is also not clear whether they are objects to identify — merge — with or to separate form, just as it is never clear whether the parts of the sculpture are merging or separating. Shapiro's sculptures are fraught with conflict, even when they seem like ironical plays on the idea of sculptural "integrity," as in the pedestal pieces JS 391A (Pl. 5), JS 793 (Pl. 24) and JS 865 (Pl. 25). The leg a Shapiro sculpture stands on can be read as a residual pedestal, sardonically locating the sculpture in an "aesthetic" space of its own. Modern sculpture eliminated the pedestal to create continuity between the sculpture and surrounding space; but the pedestal — the "foot" of the sculpture — is always implicit, as a signifier of the place the sculpture freely stands. The fact that it is possible to read the part of Shapiro's sculpture that stands on the ground as a prosthetic pedestal as well as regard it as simply another odd sculptural part, suggests the convergence of the traditional and modern purposes of sculpture, or rather their transitional relationship, in Shapiro. In the one, the pedestal elevates the sculptural figure into a mirror reflecting, in a single form, obscure feelings about our body, self, and others; in the other, the lack of pedestal gives the abstract sculpture a spatial immediacy that makes it expressively direct. As usual, at the extremes, opposites meet.

Notes

1 John Perrault, "Minimal Abstracts," *Minimalism:
   A Critical Anthology*, ed. Gregory Battcock
   (New York: E.P. Dutton, 1968), p. 259.

2 John Dewey, *The Quest for Certainty* (New
   York: Minton, Balch, 1929), p. 9.

3 Quoted in Herschel B. Chipp, ed., *Theories of
   Modern Art* (Berkeley: University of California
   Press, 1968), pp., 263, 264, 265.

4 D. W. Winnicott, "Transitional Objects and
   Transitional Phenomena" (1951), *Collected
   Papers, Through Paediatrics to Psycho-Analysis*
   (London: Tavistock, 1958), p. 239.

5 Georg Groddeck, "Language," *The Meaning of
   Illness* (New York: International Universities
   Press, 1977), p. 249.

6 See Gaston Bachelard, *The Poetics of Space*
   (Boston: Beacon Press, 1969), chapters 7-9.

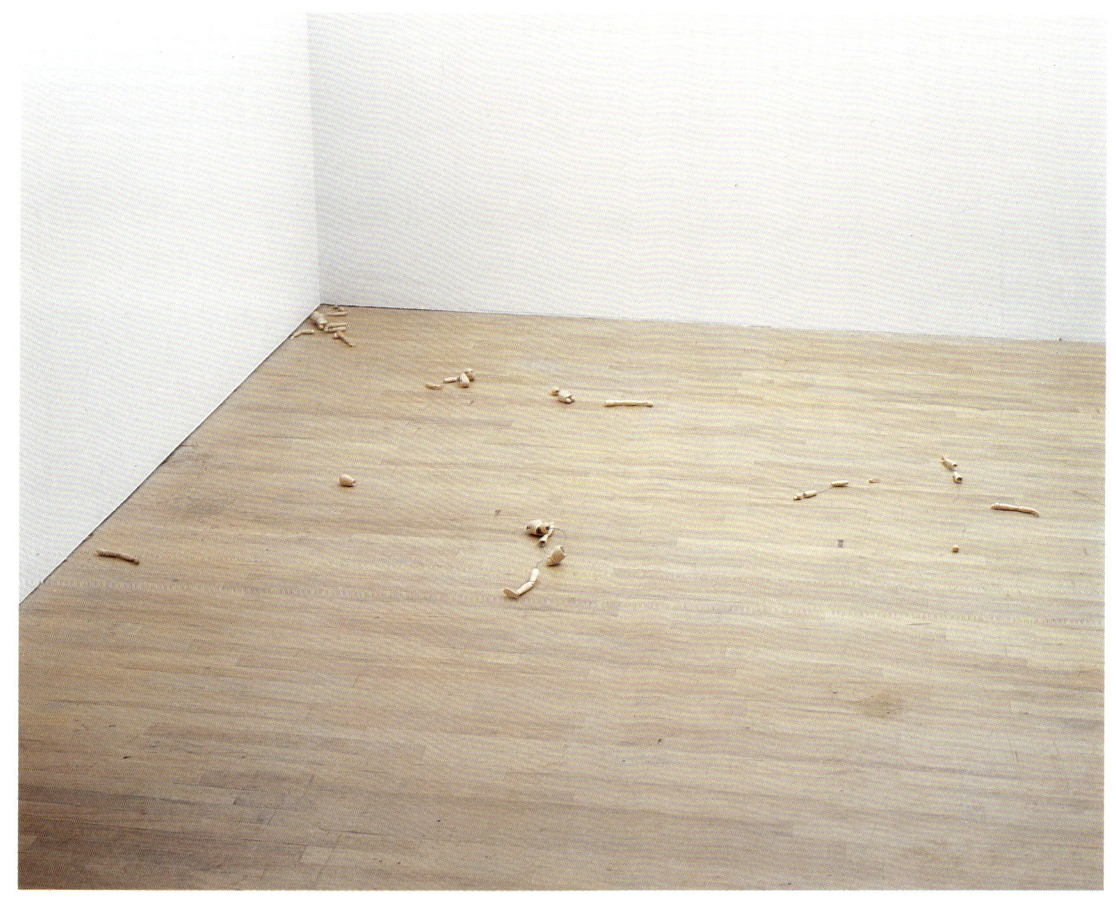

Plate 2   Untitled, 1974 (JS 920)

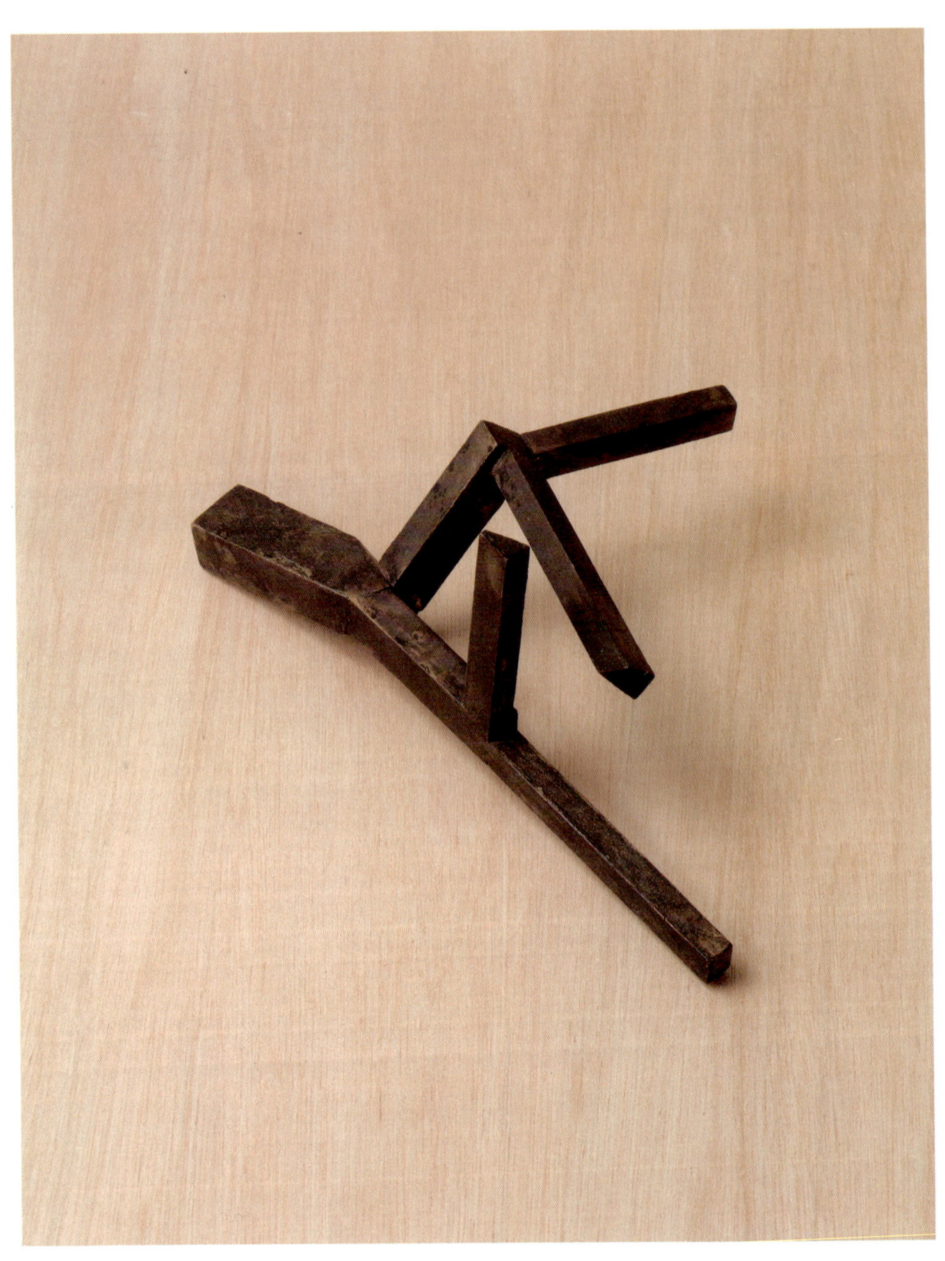

Plate 3　Untitled, 1976-77 (JS 155)

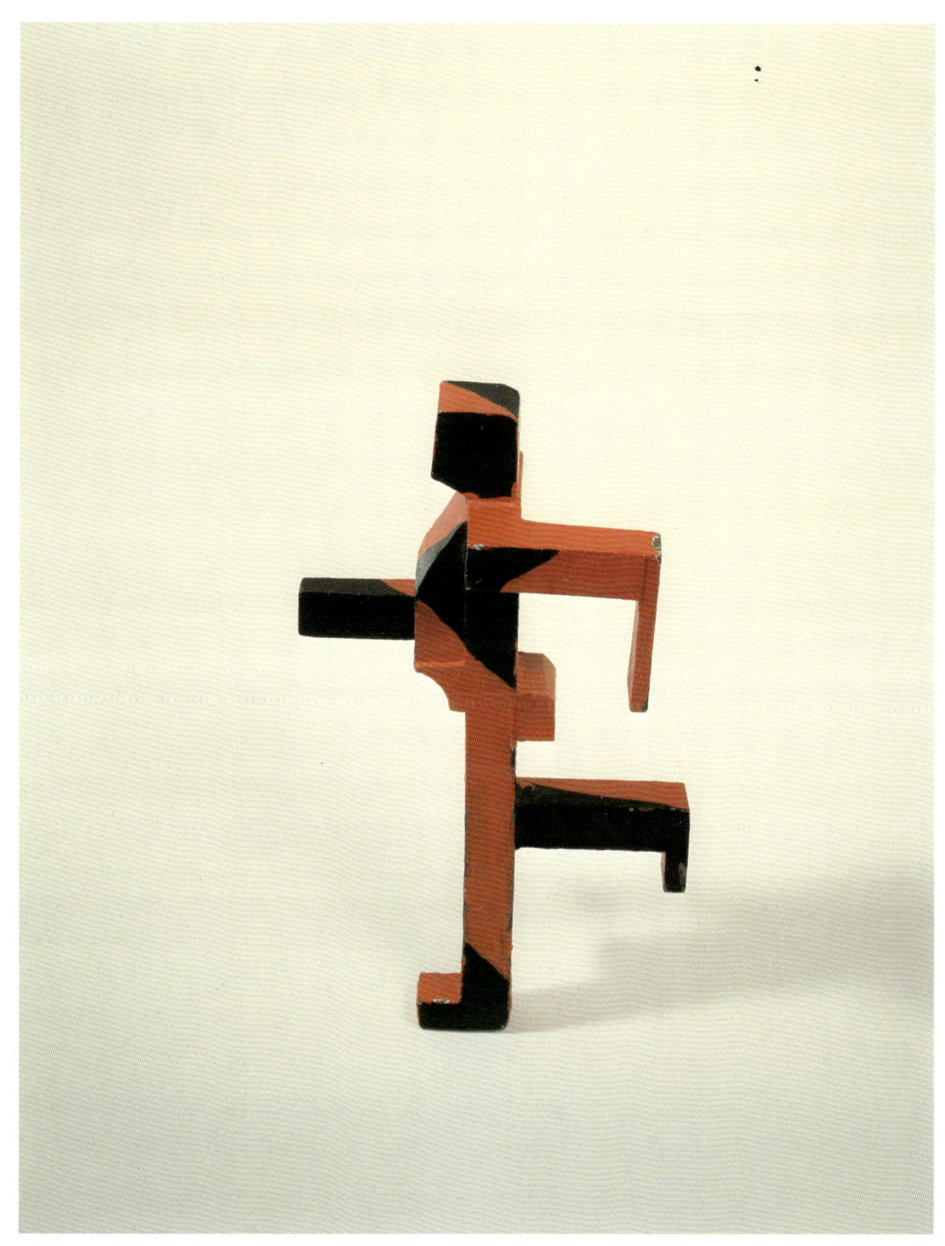

Plate 4   Untitled, 1976-77 (JS 167A)

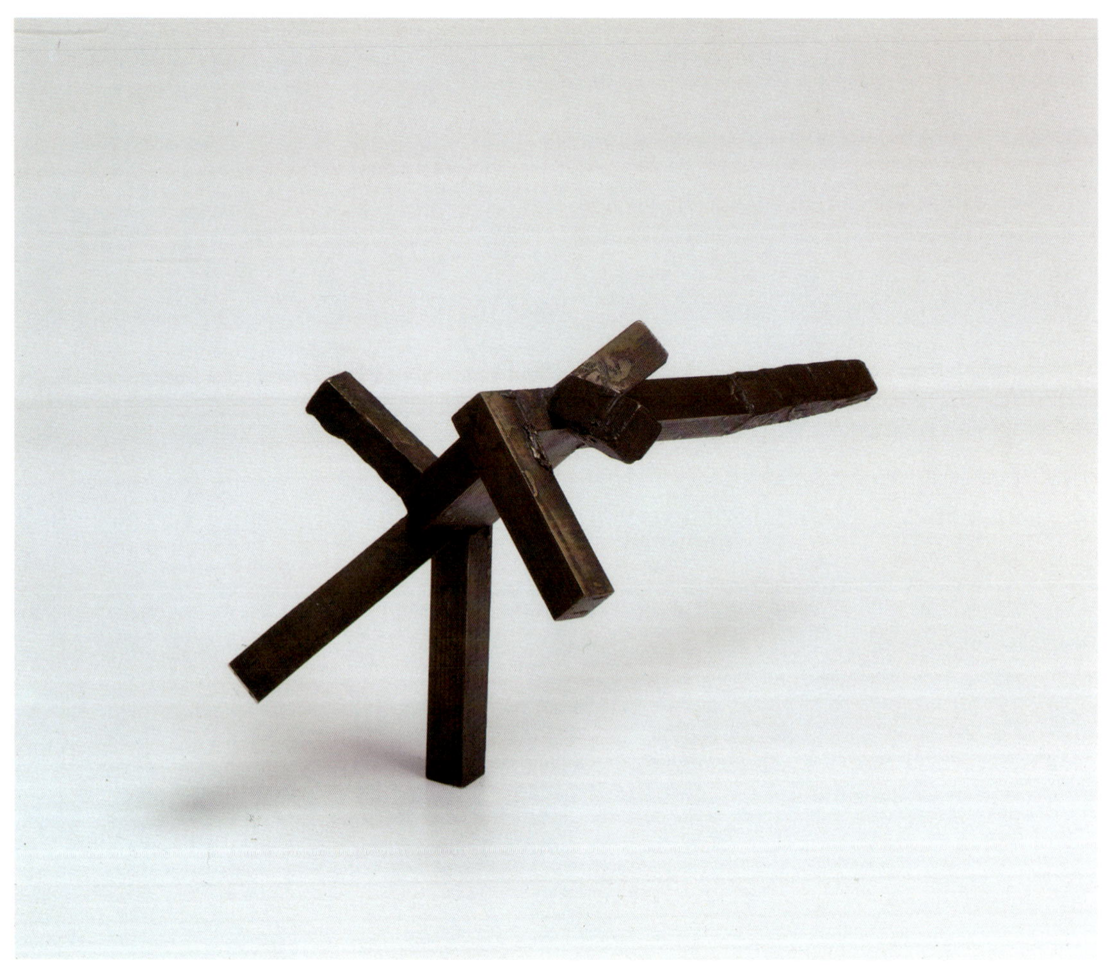

Plate 5   Untitled, 1980-82 (JS 391A)

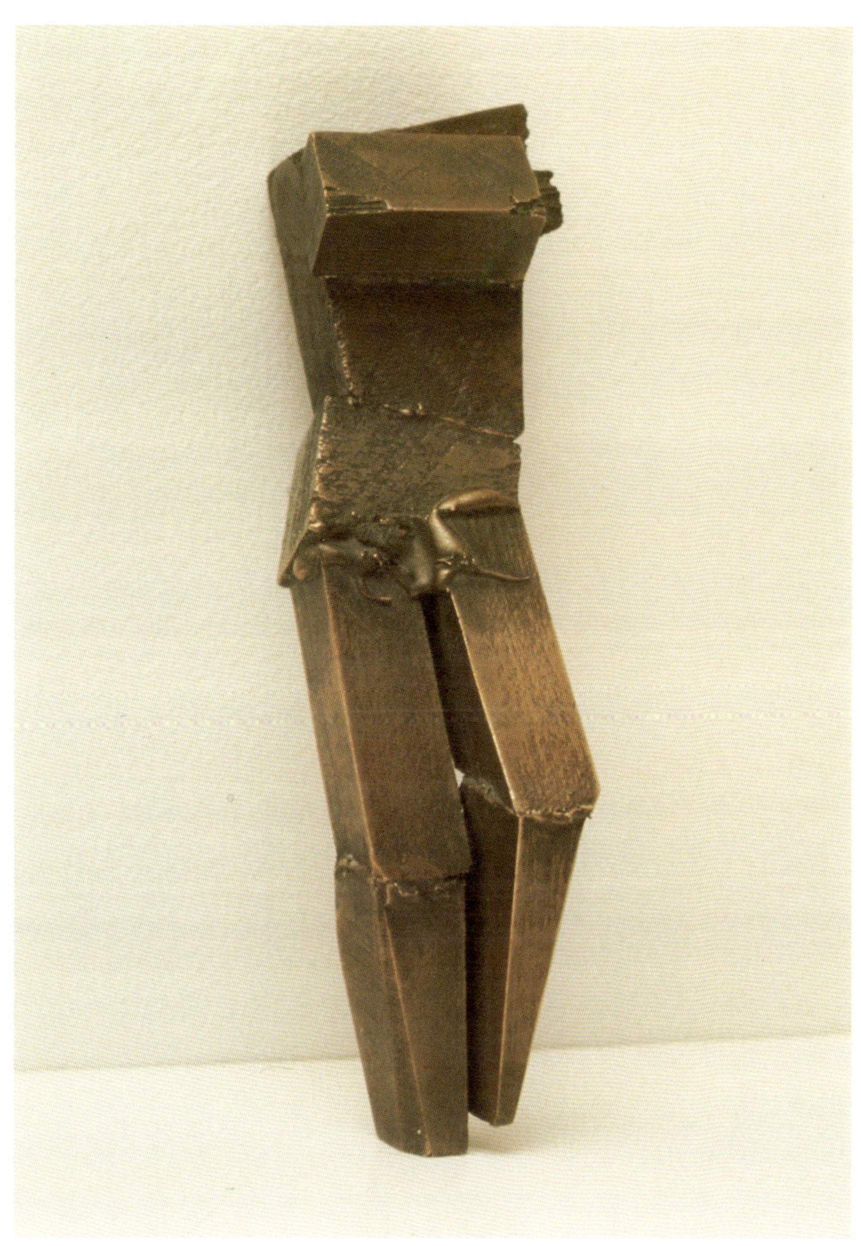

Plate 6　Untitled, 1979-82 (JS 383A)

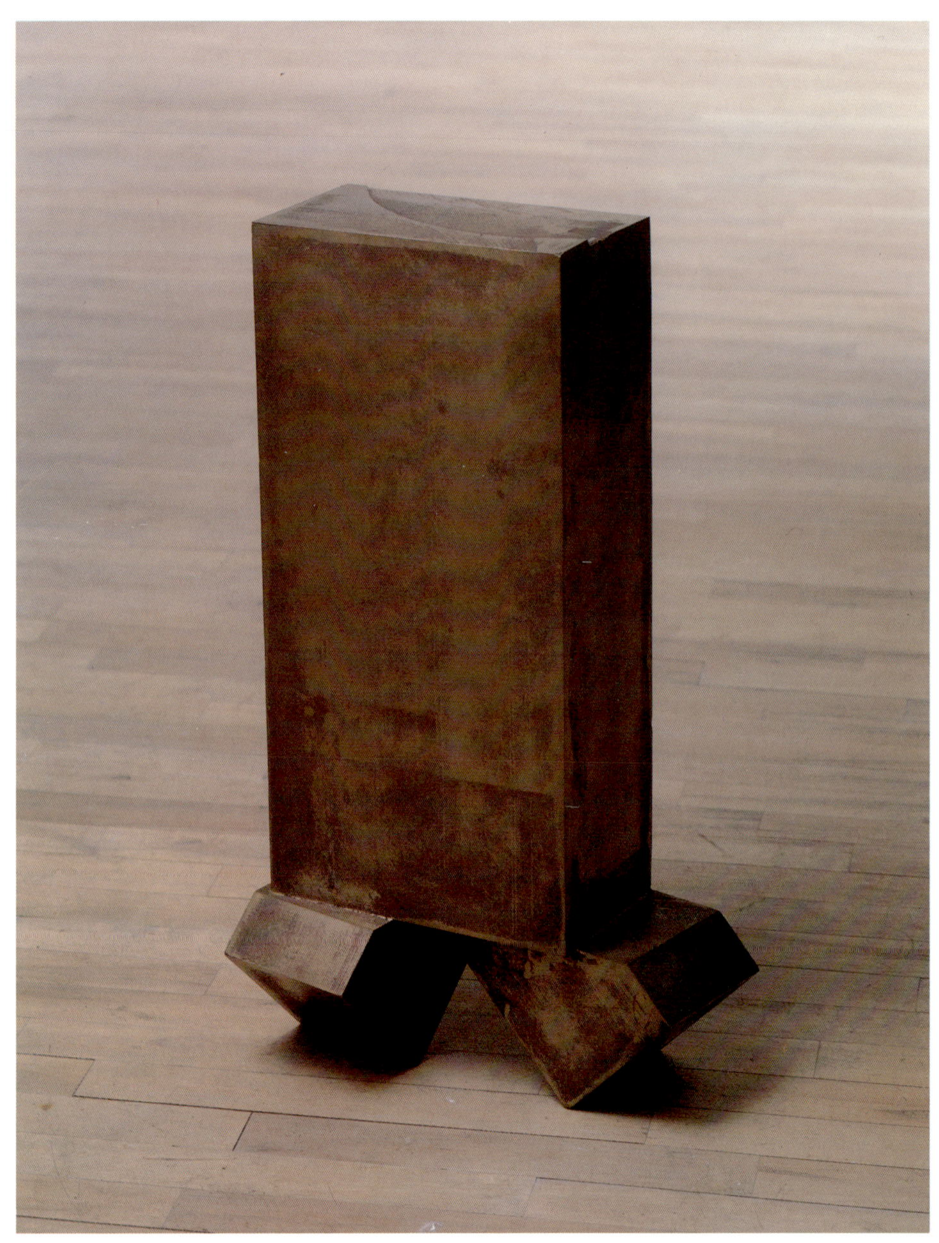

Plate 7   Untitled, 1982 (JS 465)

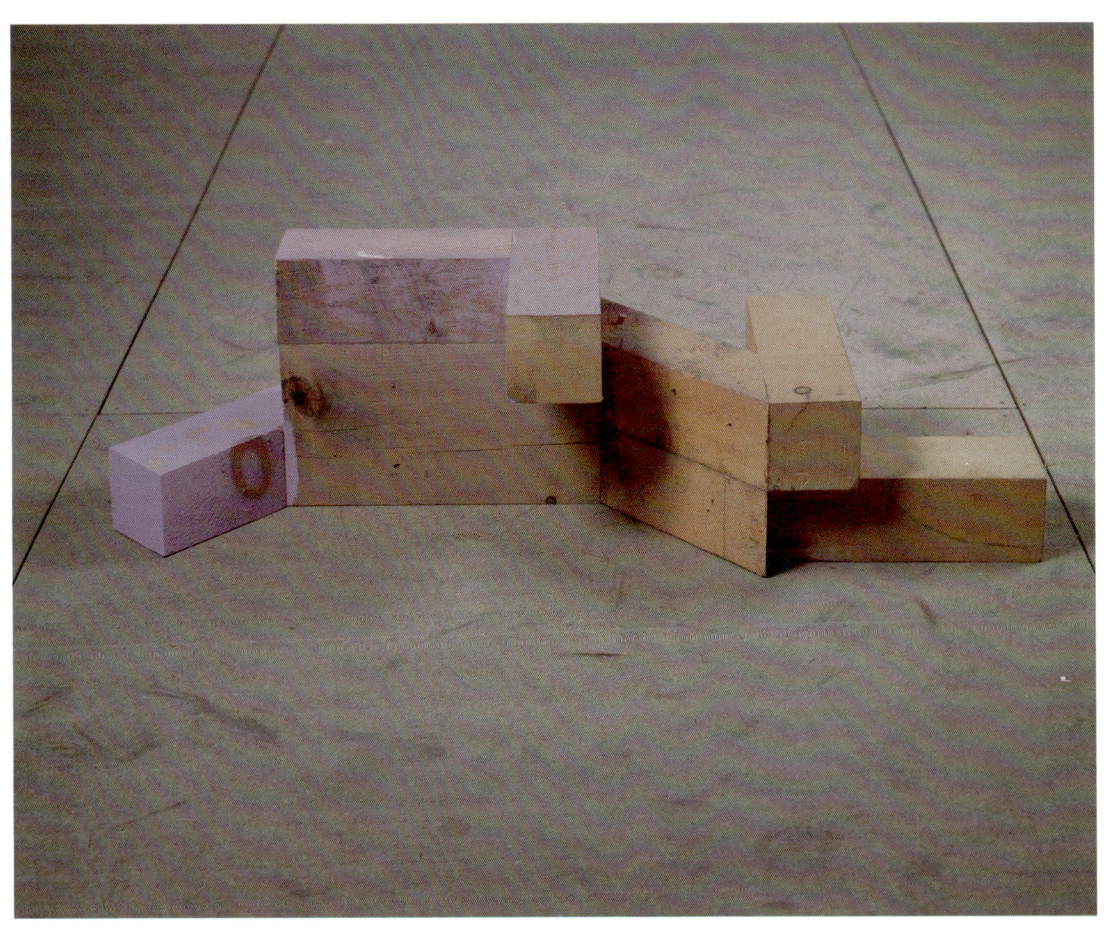

Plate 8   Untitled, 1982 (JS 466)

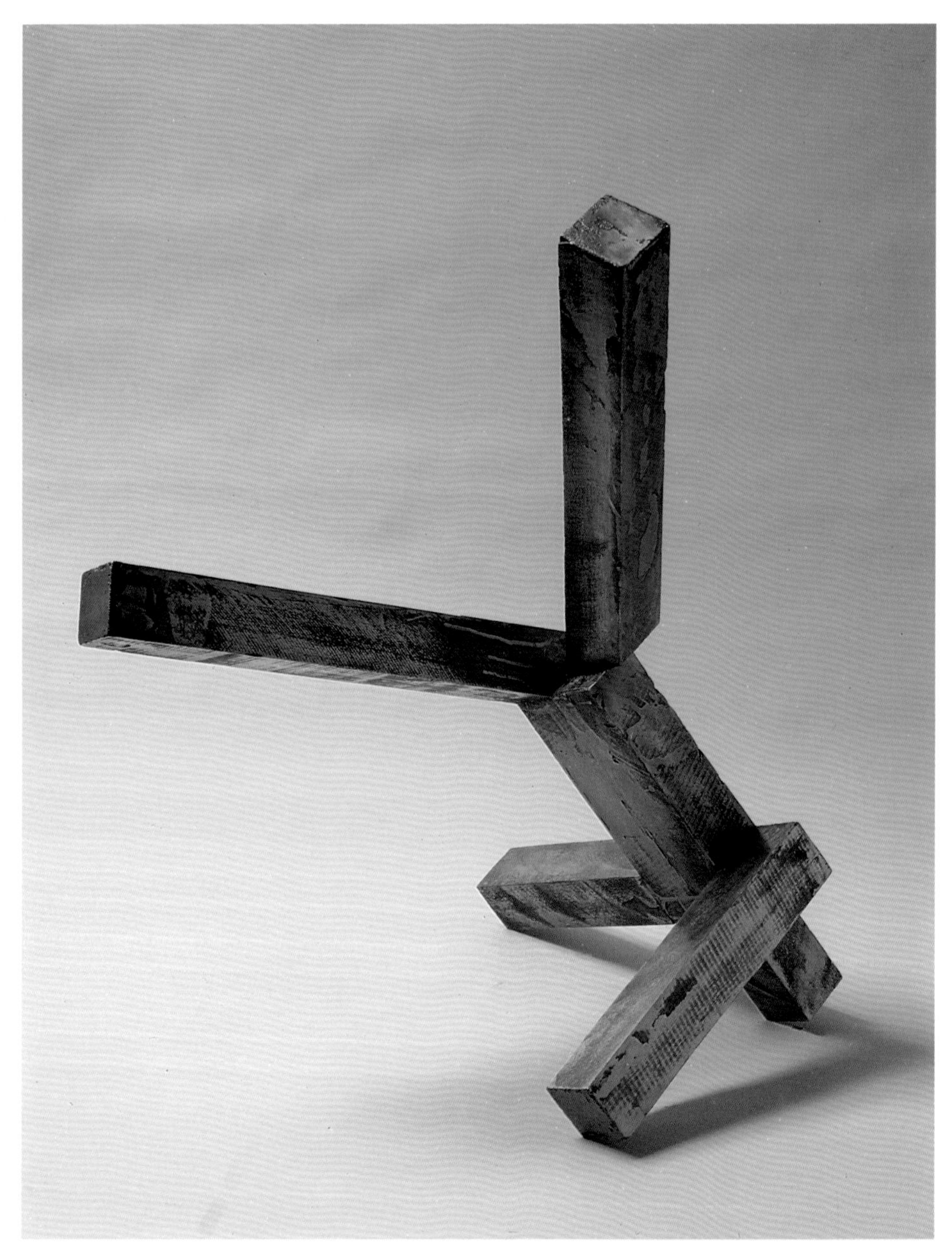

Plate 9   Untitled, 1980-82 (JS 467)

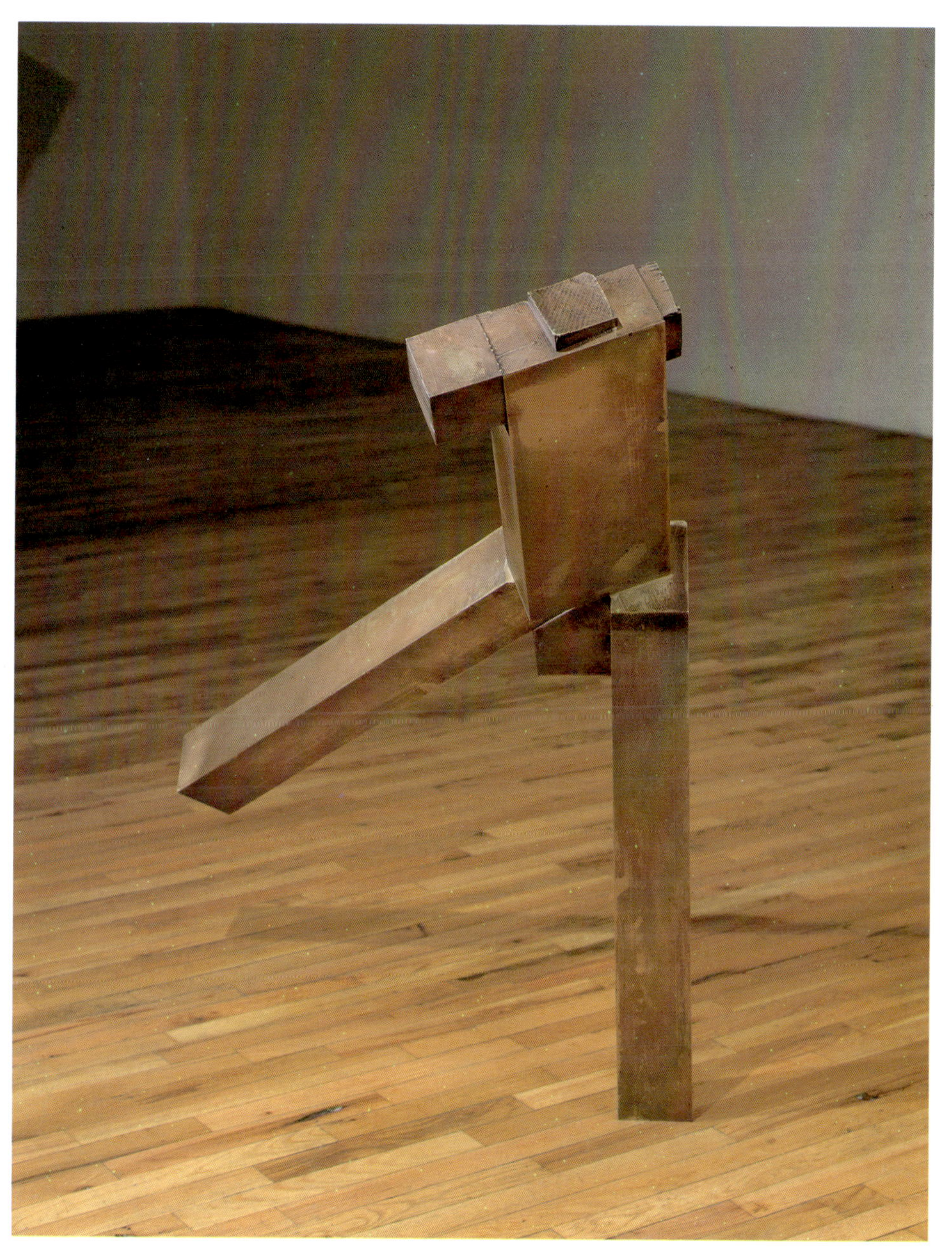

Plate 10   Untitled, 1982-83 (JS 497)

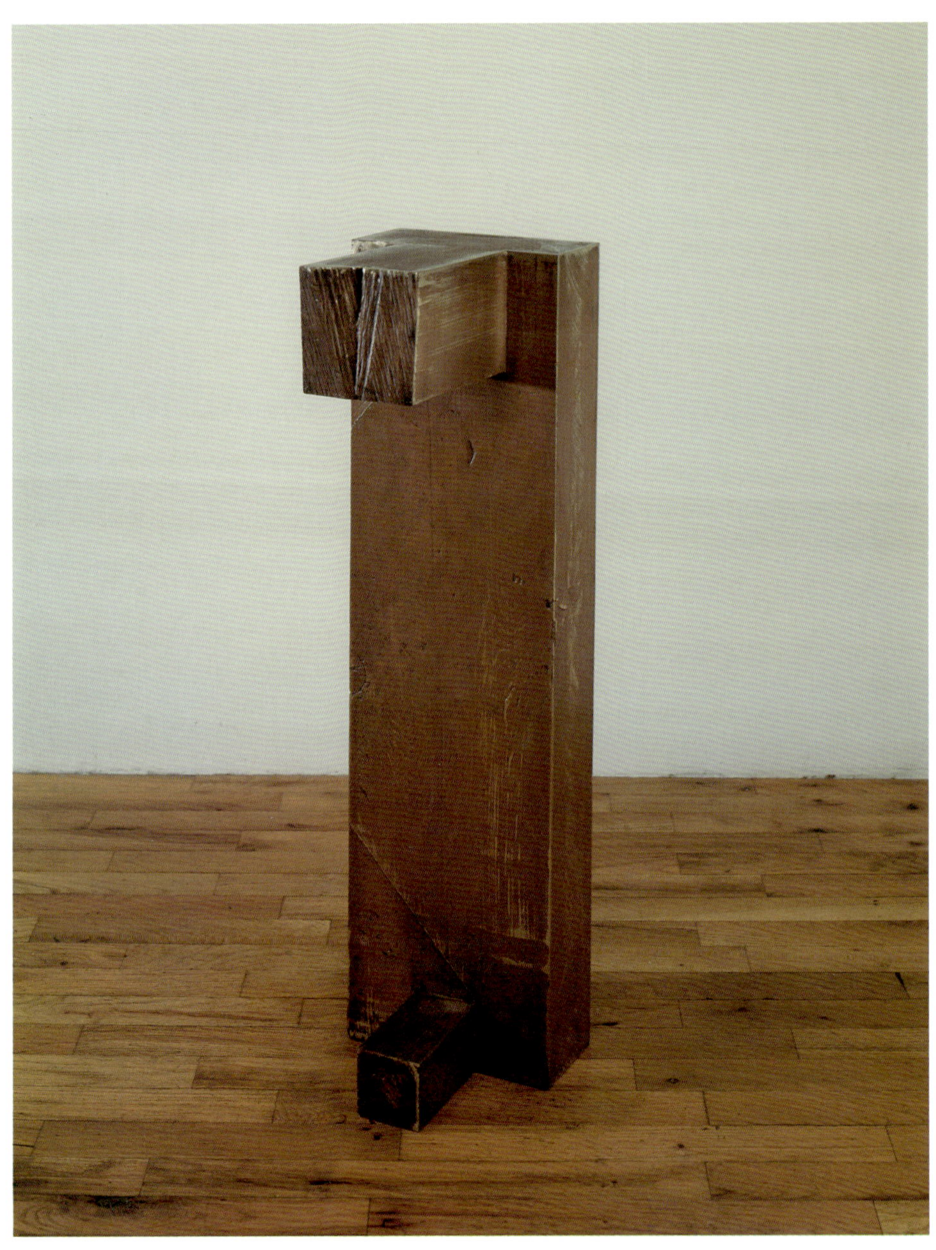

Plate 11   Untitled, 1983-84 (JS 584)

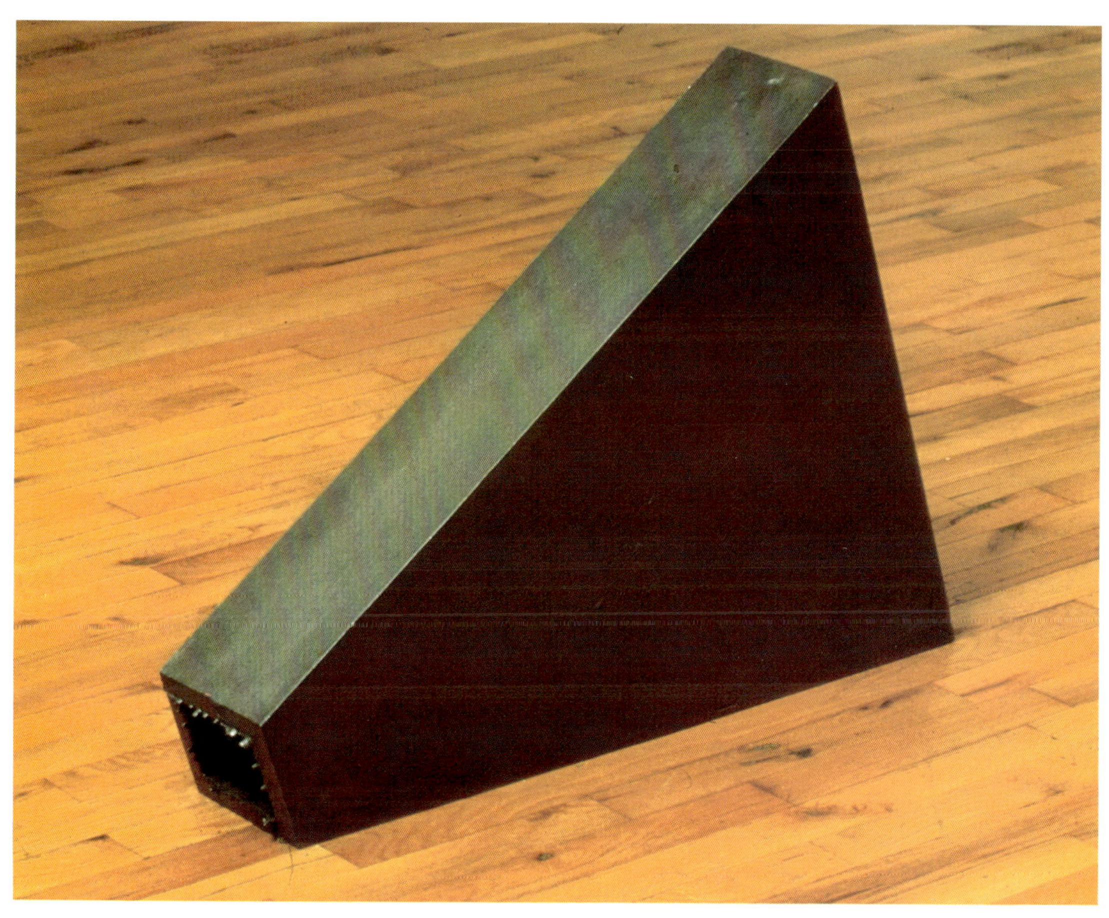

Plate 12   Untitled, 1984 (JS 587)

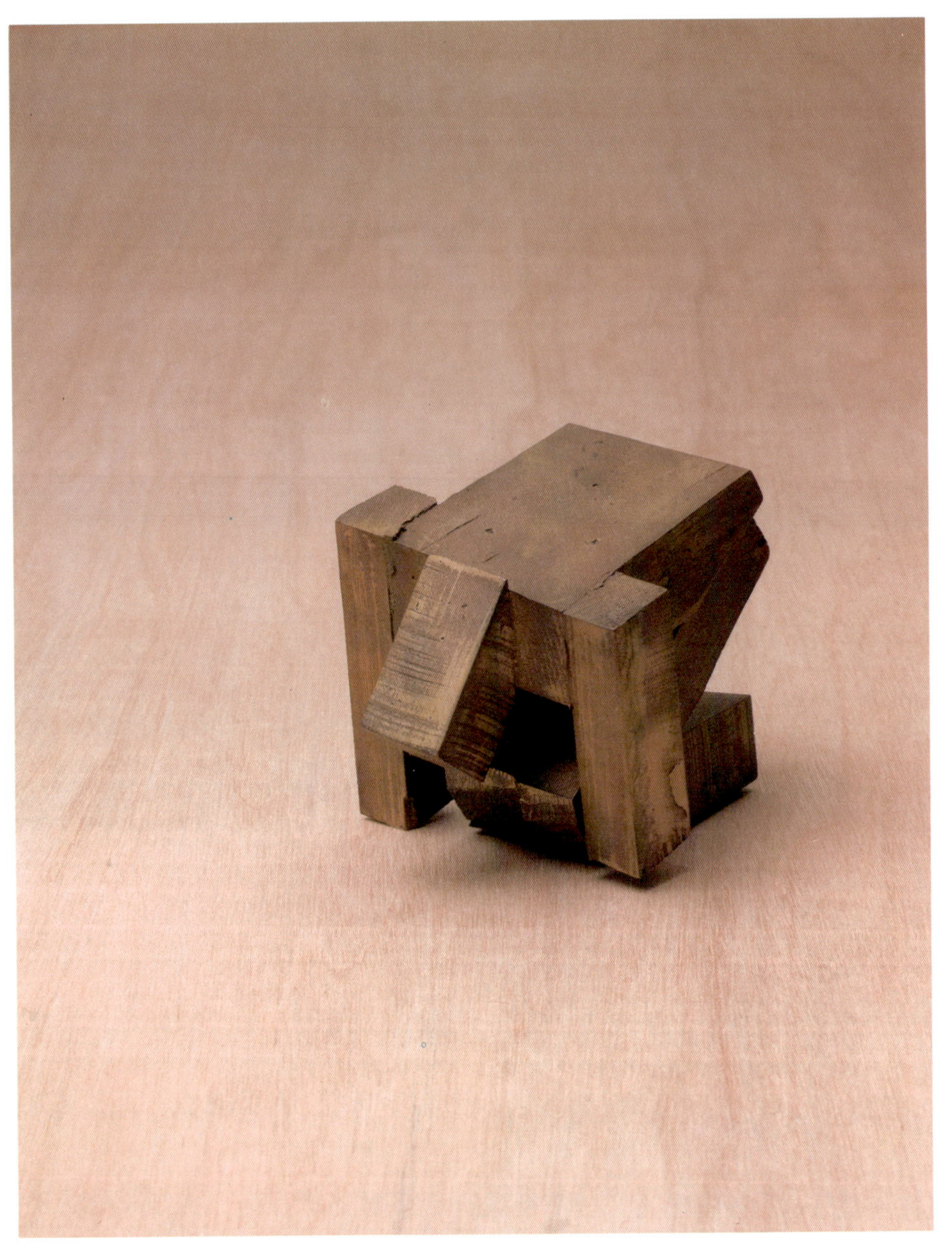

Plate 13   Untitled, 1982-84 (JS 593)

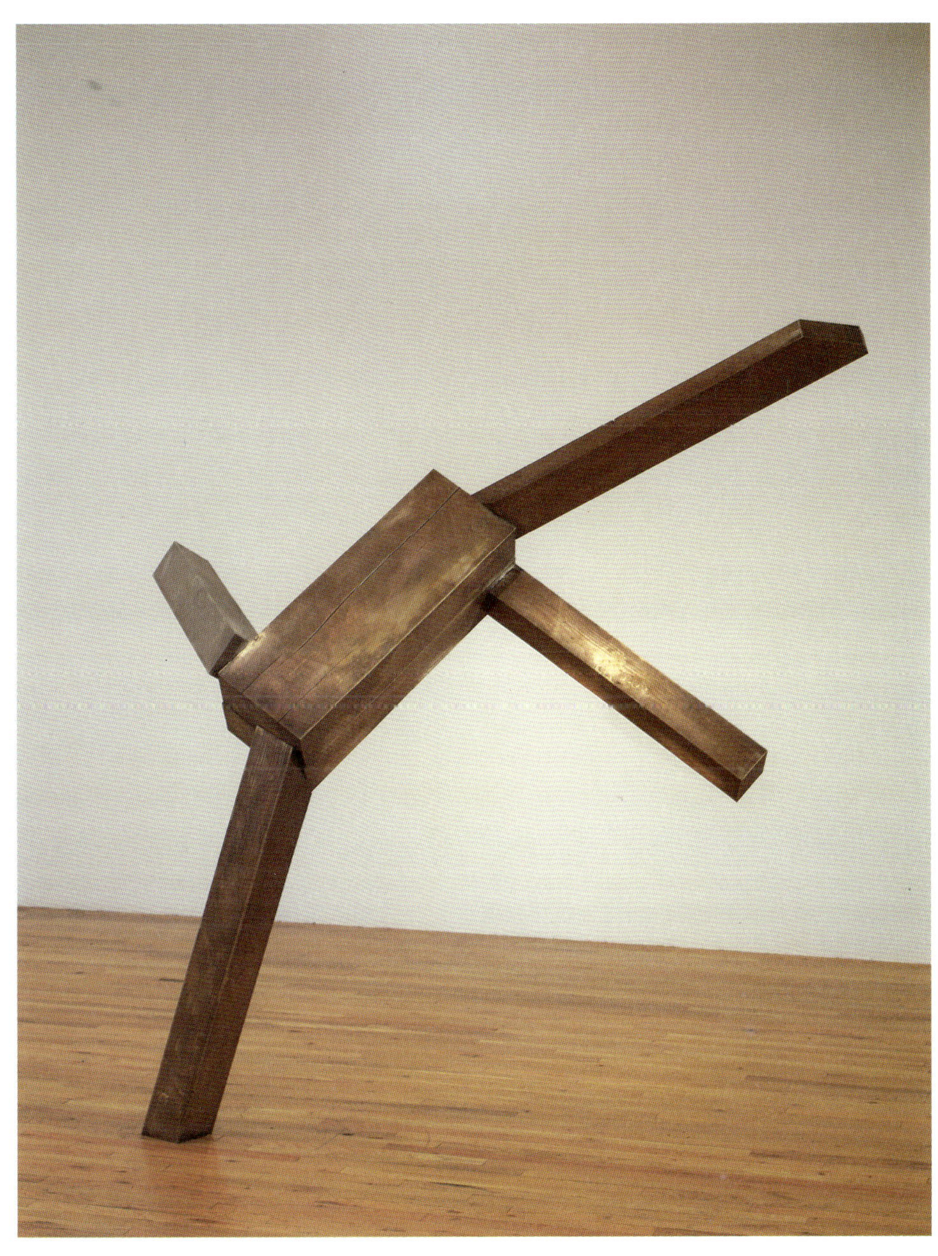

Plate 14   Untitled, 1983-84 (JS 595)

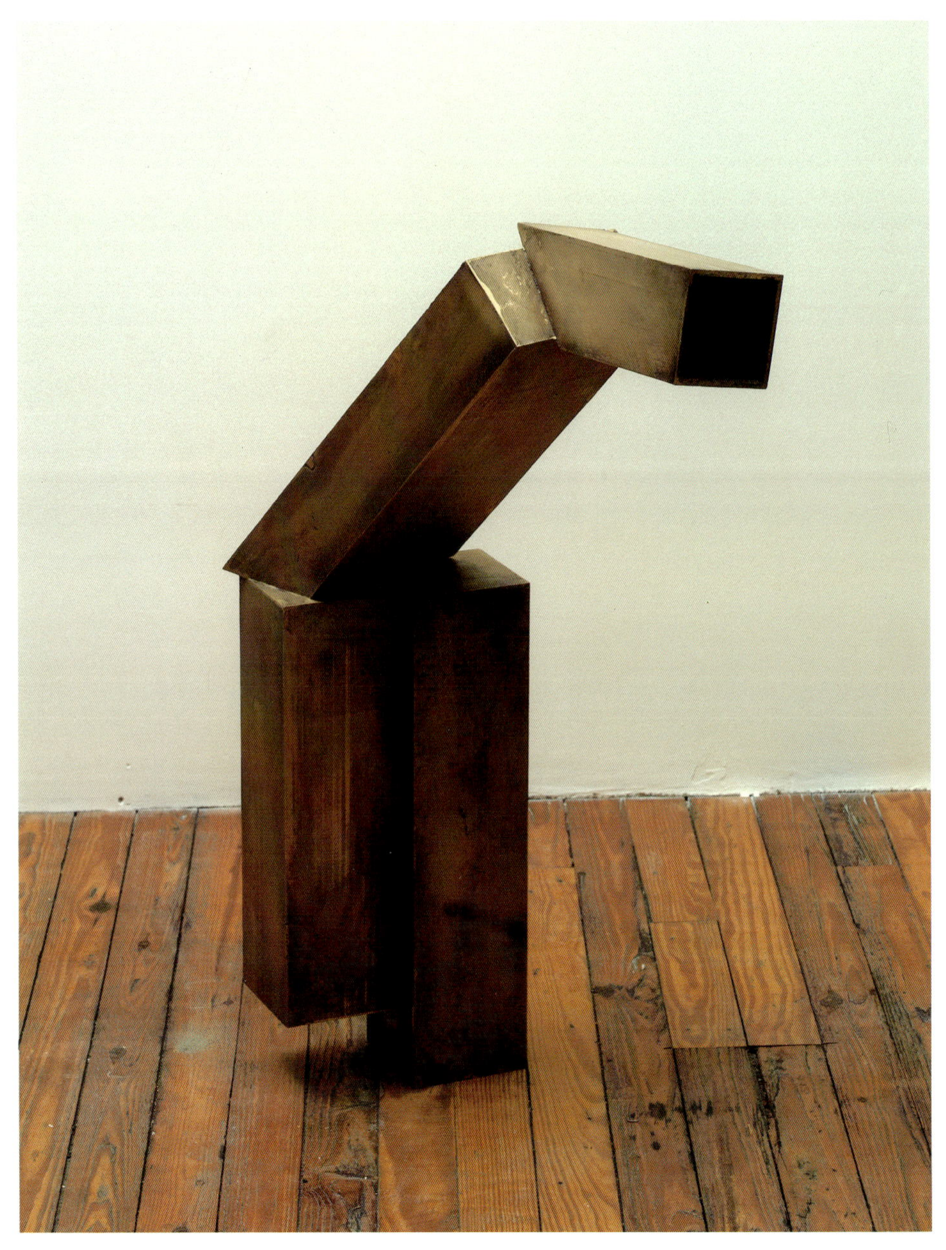

Plate 15   Untitled, 1985 (JS 612)

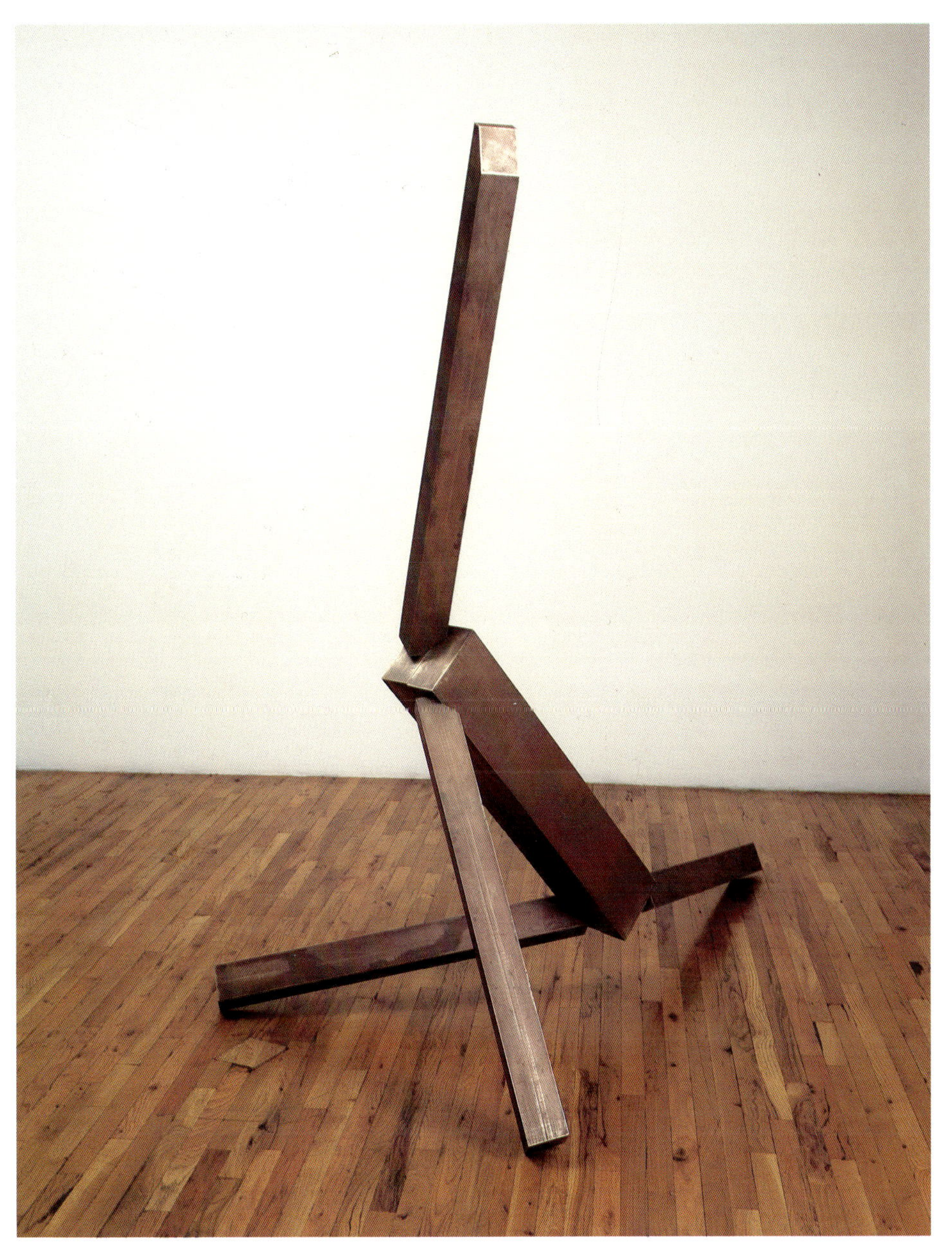

Plate 16   Untitled, 1985 (JS 624)

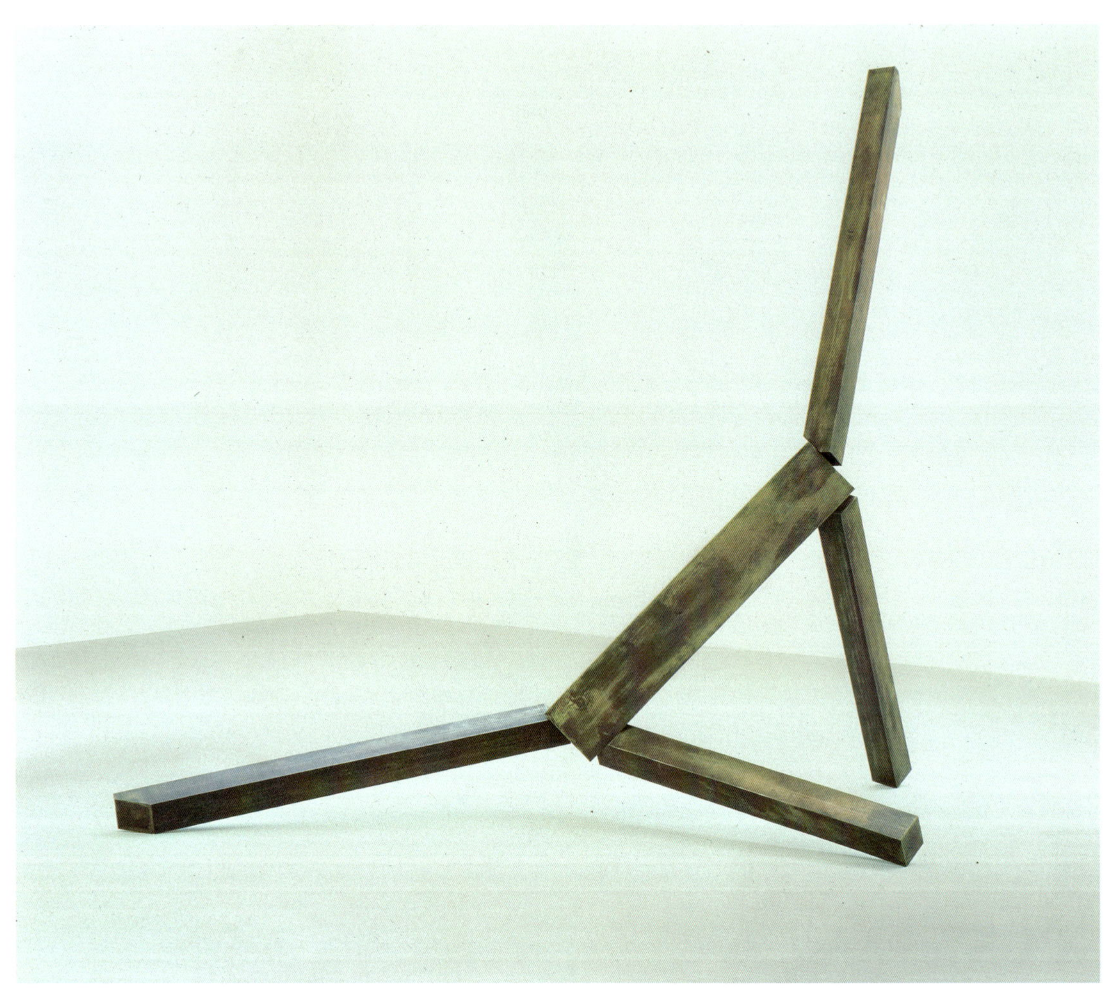

Plate 17   Untitled, 1985 (JS 625)

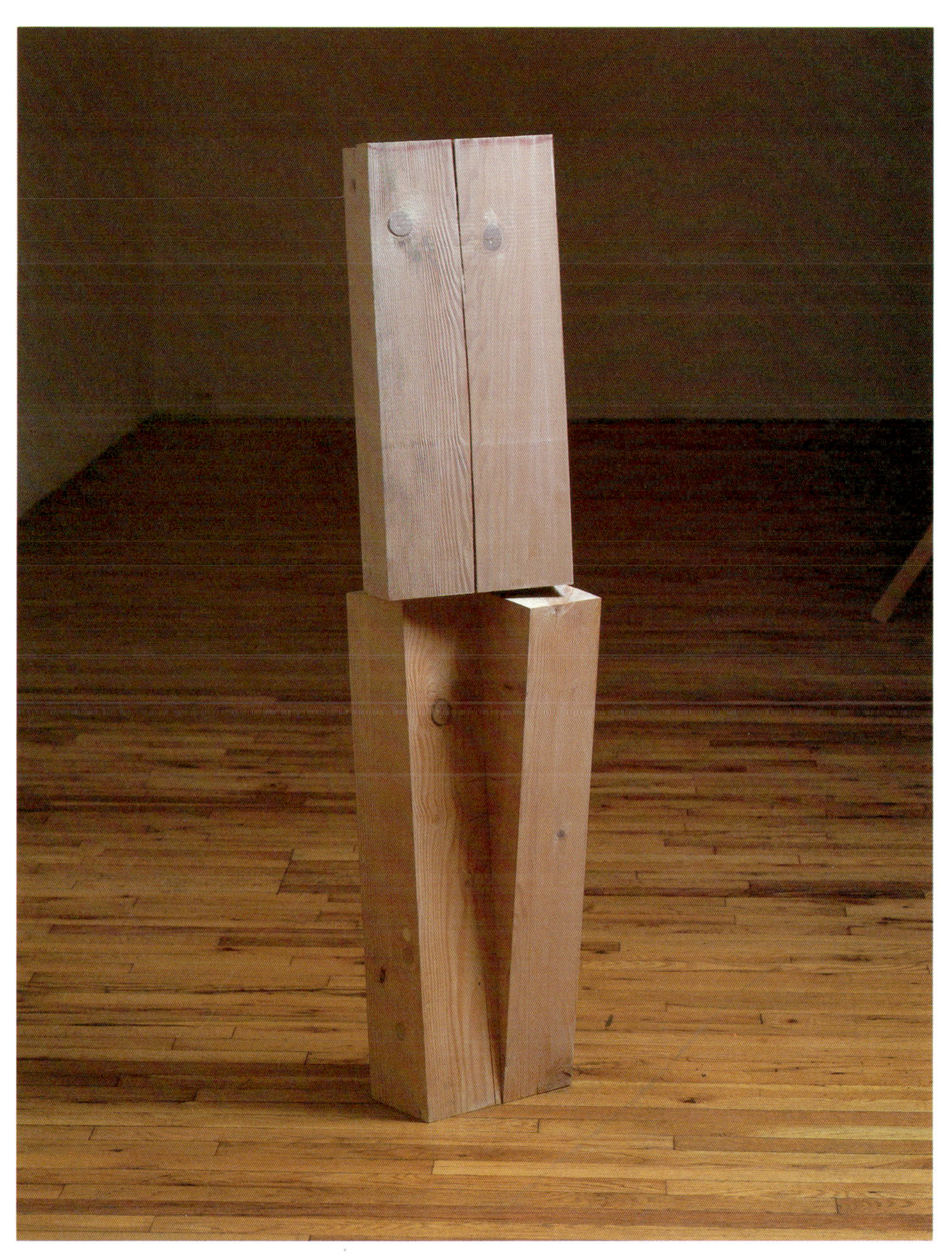

Plate18   Untitled, 1986 (JS 712)

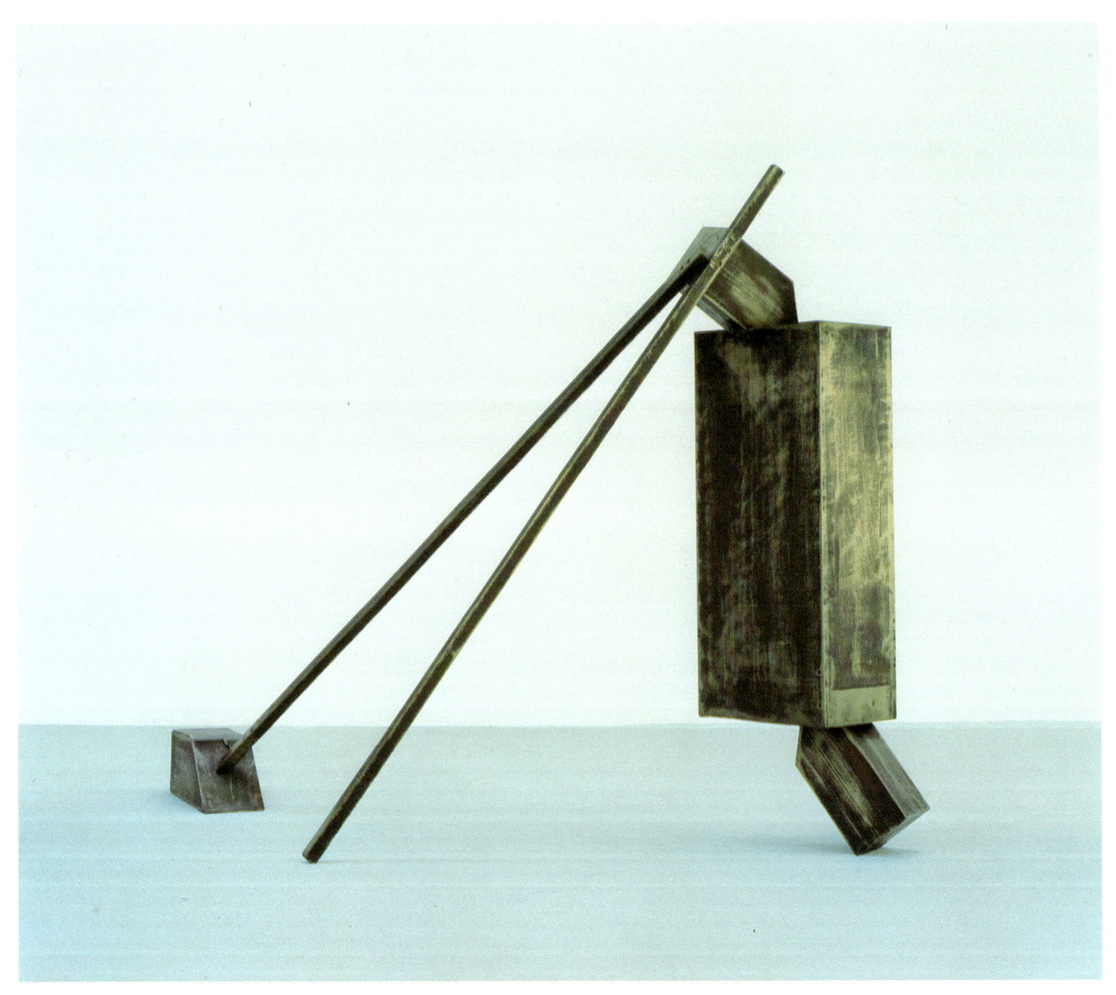

Plate 19   Untitled, 1986 (JS 720)

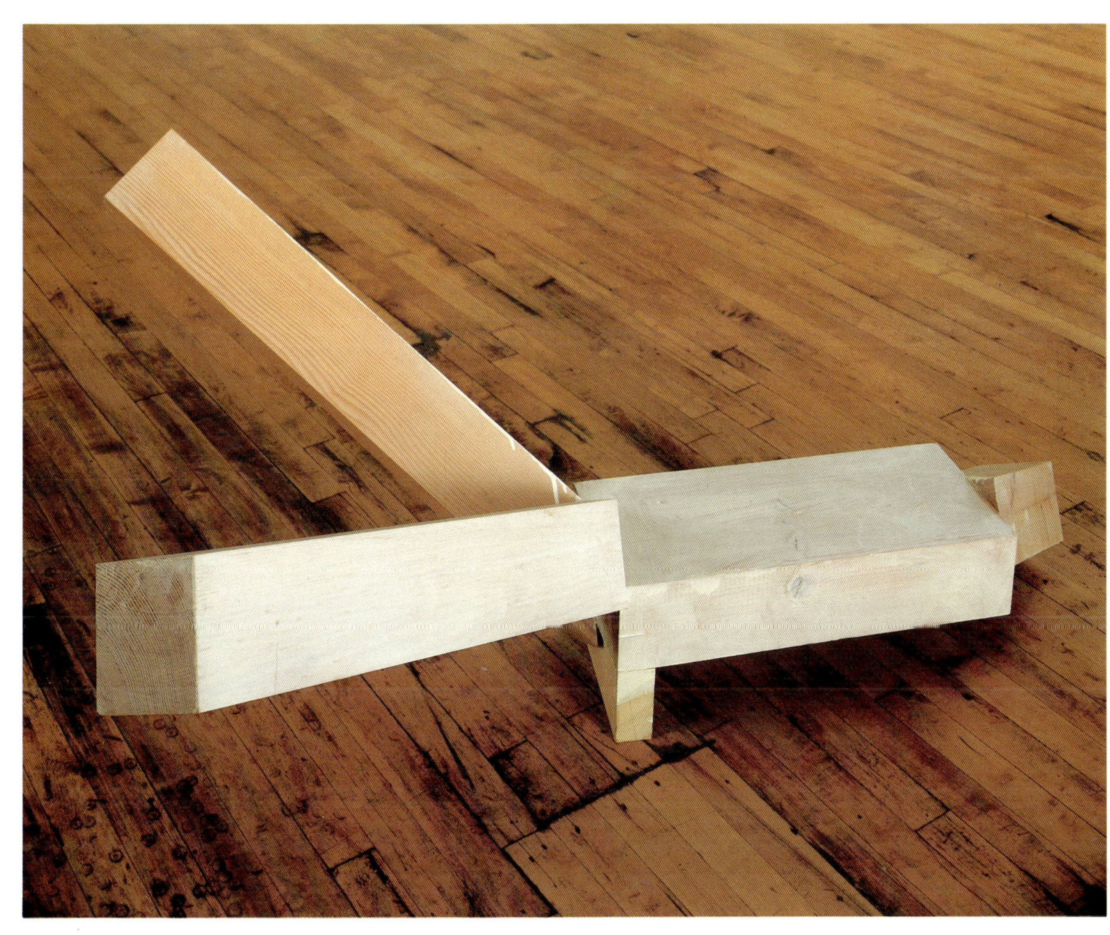

Plate 20   Untitled, 1987 (JS 735)

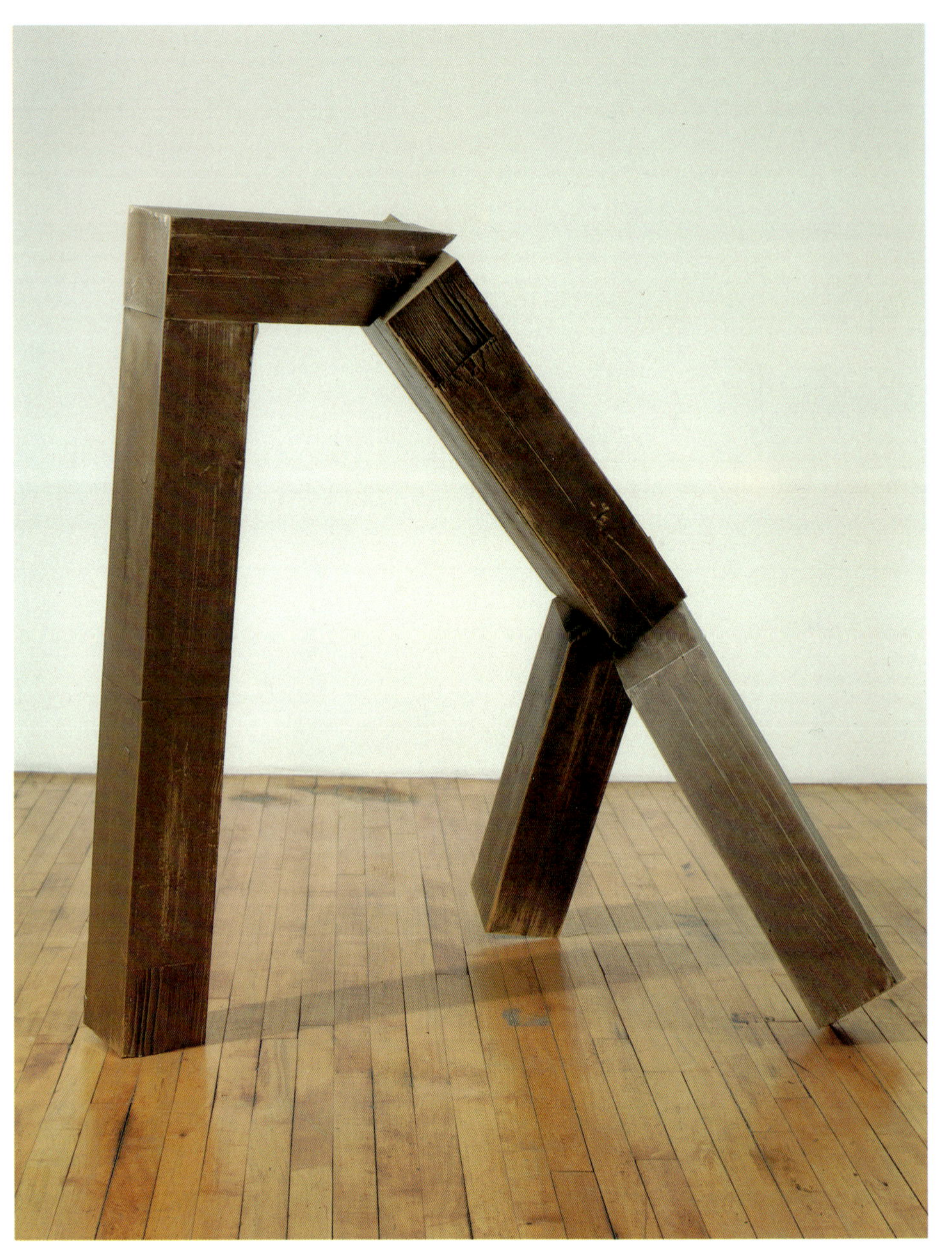

Plate 21   Untitled, 1987 (JS 766)

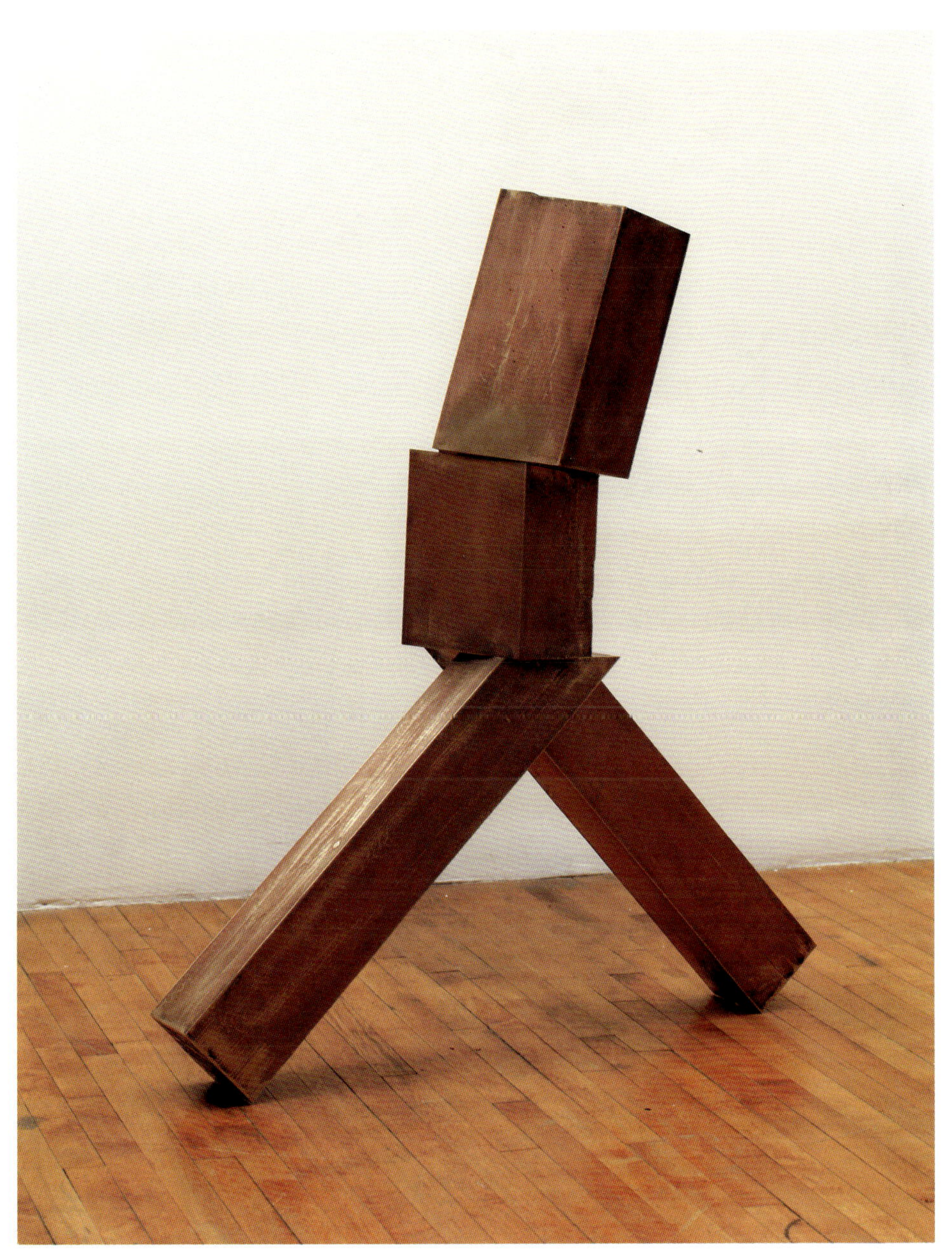

Plate 22   Untitled, 1987 (JS 767)

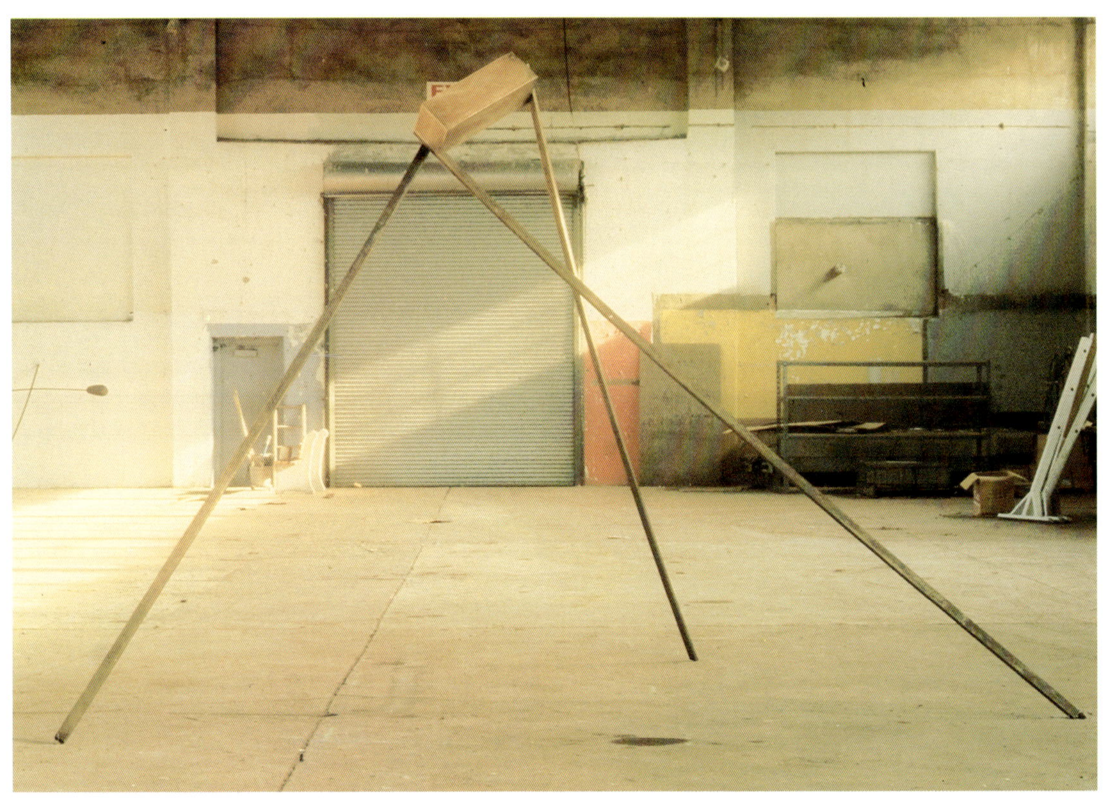

Plate 23   Untitled, 1987-88 (JS 790)

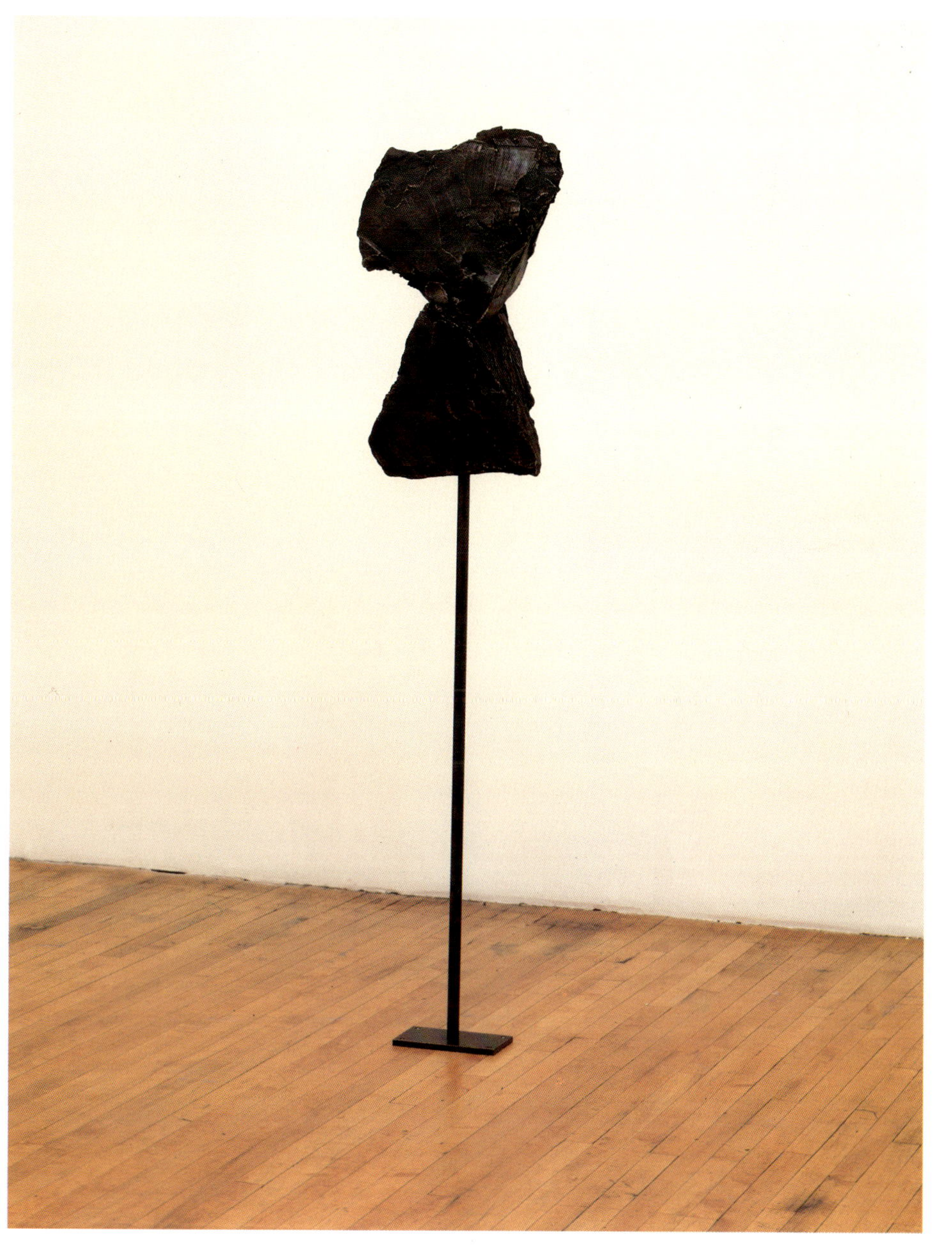

Plate 24   Untitled, 1987-88 (JS 793)

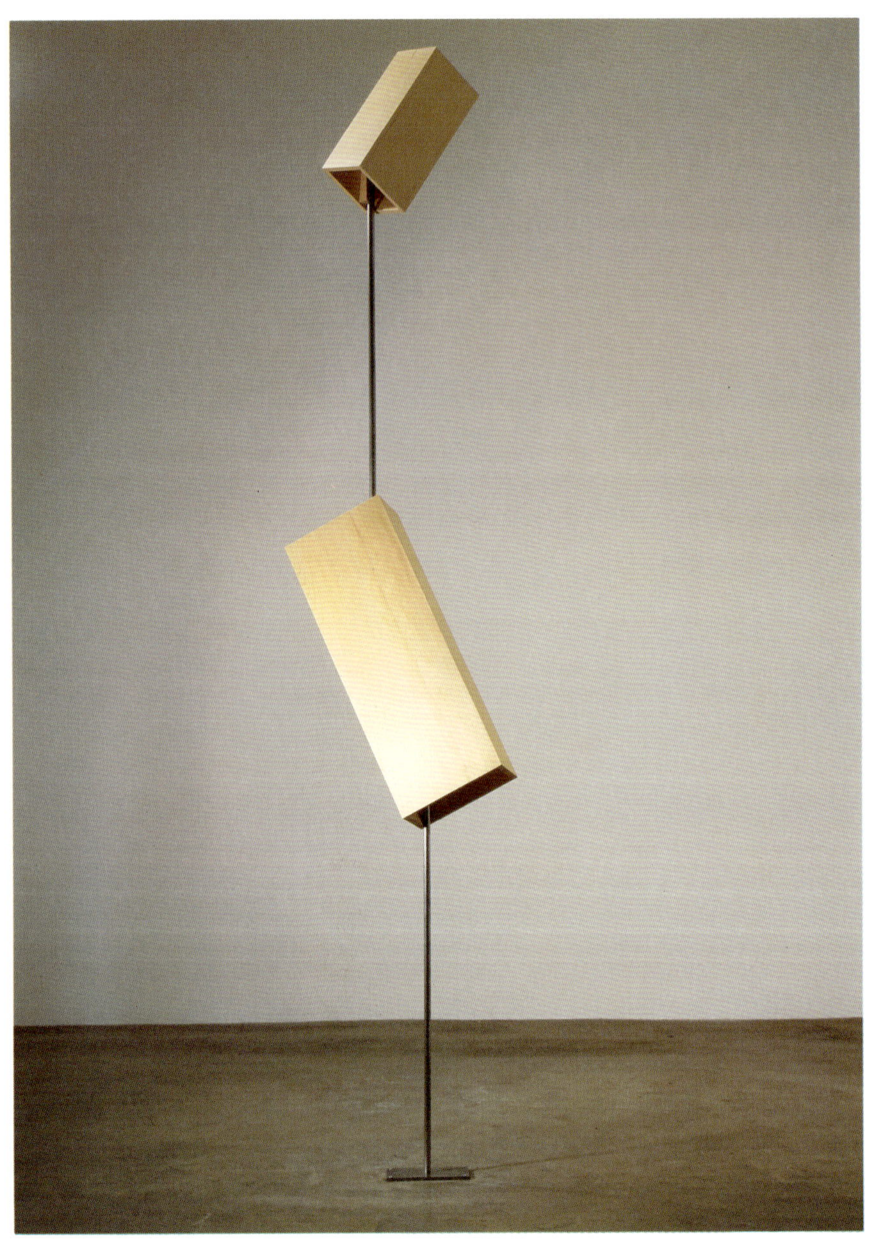

Plate 25   Untitled, 1988 (JS 865)

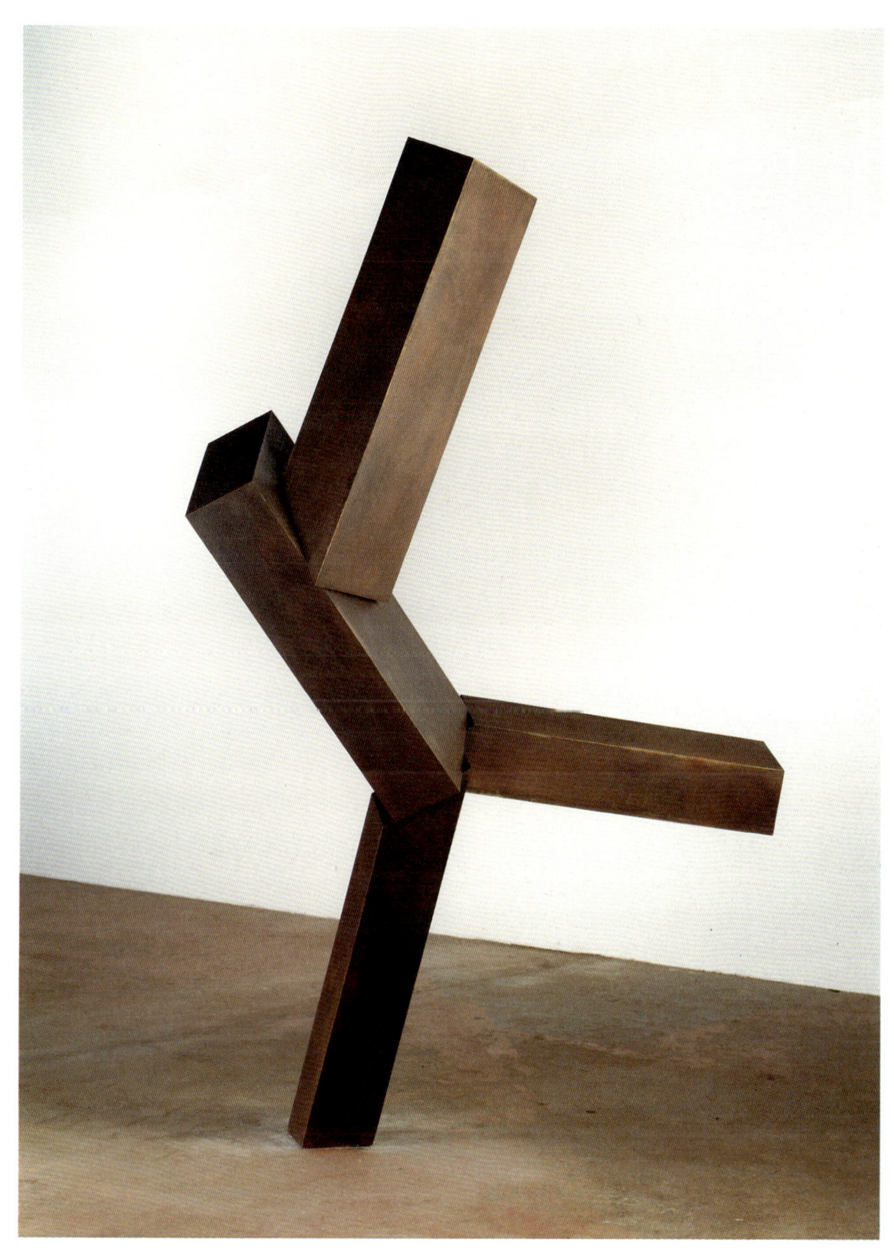

Plate 26   Untitled, 1989 (JS 909)

Interview

Deborah Leveton

This interview with Joel Shapiro was conducted
by Deborah Leveton, Associate Curator of
the Des Moines Art Center, in the artist's studio
in New York City, January 2 and 3, 1990, while
looking at images of the sculptures to be included
in the exhibition. The interview was edited by
Sarah McFadden and Joan Simon.

 To put the sculptures in this exhibition in context:
Shapiro's works of the late 1960s and early 1970s
were process-oriented or involved with issues of
psychology and memory that referred to the human
condition through the absence of the figure. He
created his first sculpture with explicit inclusion of
the figure in 1972. His first free-standing wood
figure sculpture was made in 1976-77, and his first
large-scale figures were completed in 1981.

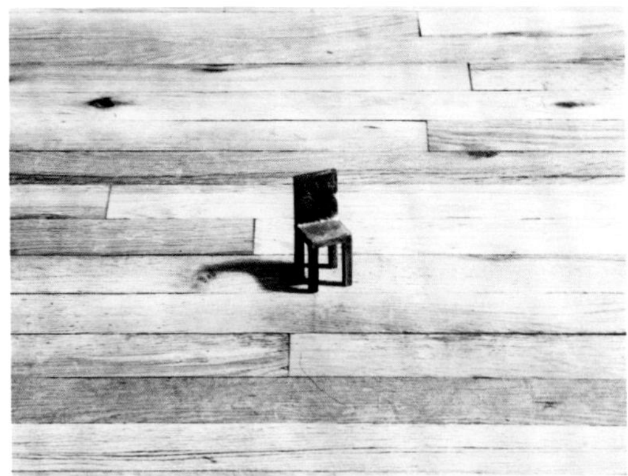

Fig. 1　Untitled, 1973-74 (JS 64)

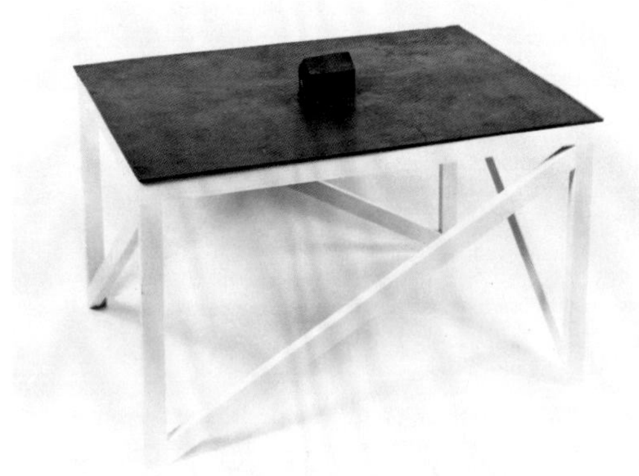

Fig. 2　Untitled, 1975-76, (JS 151)

Deborah Leveton: In your early works, like the chair or the house, you implied the presence of the figure through its absence (Figs. 1 and 2). What made you admit the figure?

Joel Shapiro: I think there was a point in the mid-70s when I felt that there were certain things I could not achieve unless I began to deal with them more directly.

Such as?

Certain emotions. For example, in the pieces where there was a tiny aperture in a small obdurate mass or the small isolated chair. These pieces carried a lot of emotion. They were very psychologi-cal, very magical. About memory and sorrow.

Although by the time I was working with the houses, I began to feel like I had isolated a metaphor. I felt that I had understood the issues involved; the formal issues plus the psychological issues seemed clearer. There was really no other place to go with that. So I began to want to make sculpture that functioned more in the present where you really were not involved with issues of memory. I wanted sculptures that physically functioned in the room, in the space we occupy, not in projective space.

The way some of these subsequent pieces literally engage the space around them, you can't refute their presence. You don't have to enter into a psychological or magical world in order to participate with the work. The work is there, in the present, active. That really began with the more figurative work.

The change in your work took place around 1976-77?

I'll show you an important piece from that time which is very figurative (JS 155, Pl. 3). It referred to a tree, but it also had an explicit reference to the human figure. Another difference was that the work became additive. If you are going to deal with the figure, you have to take parts and put them together. I was never interested in representational imagery, doing a portrait or a full figure. I was much more interested, and still am interested, in the psychology of the form. I don't think there was a tremendous difference in my interest from the early work, the more architectural work. It was just a different means of getting there, a more real, present means.

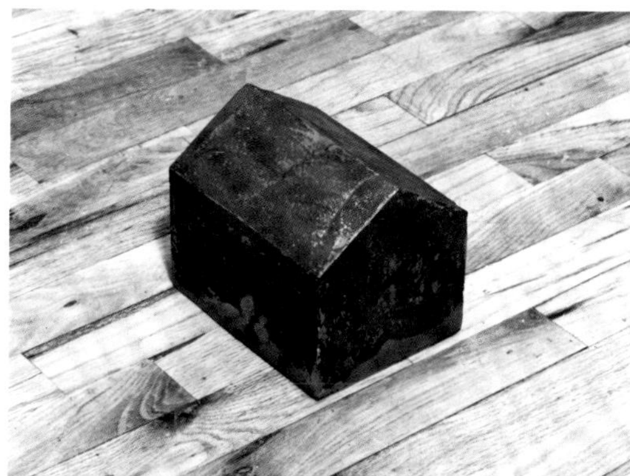

Fig. 3   Untitled, 1973-74 (JS 78)

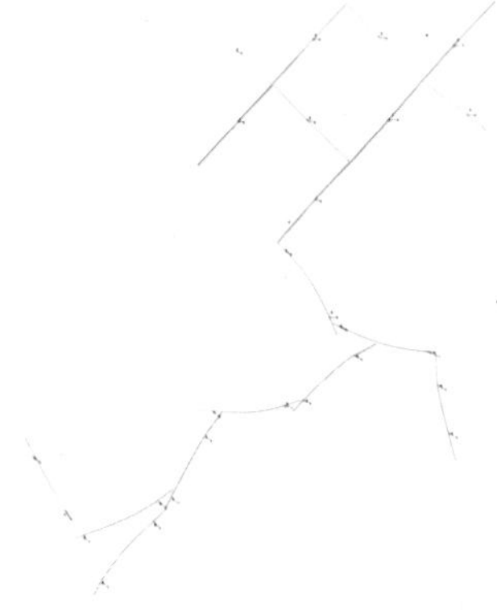

Fig. 4   *Tree*, 1973 (JS 55A)

You look at a small single house on the floor that I did (JS 78, Fig. 3) — and it would attempt to engage the space around it, where I think some of these newer pieces do engage the space around them in a very real, physical way.

I think the early pieces were very dependent on context. I wanted work that was independent of that, and that would really function on its own; where the form itself was loaded, and its effect on space around it much more kinesthetic. There is much more activity. A piece like this (JS 151, Fig. 2), with this isolation of the house on a plane, was a highly effective piece, but it wasn't functioning the way that sculpture functions. It functioned in a more pictorial zone.

How so?

It established its own perimeter and functioned within it. Some of the pieces did things formally that were really interesting. And I think there was easy access to them. That work of mine was accepted quite rapidly, and I think one reason it was accepted had to do with the fact that it existed in a more pictorial realm, and really somehow subverted notions of sculpture. It was radical because it did subvert some preconceived notions about sculpture, which subsequently I find to be more challenging than their subversion. Not preconceptions but the

ability to realize something within that arena — within the historical parameters of sculpture — that's important.

You have a statement about the tree piece in the Whitney catalogue (JS 155, Pl. 3). You discuss it mostly in terms of imagery but you also talk about its association to a death in your family.

I did other tree pieces based on arithmetic progressions. They were also figurative — one was pinned to the wall and it had a curvy root structure (Fig. 4). I was playing with the idea. Then my sister died and I made this piece.

When you're making a piece you're participating in the making of it, its immediacy, versus the realization of a more conceptual idea. This means that what you're conscious of and what happens during the making of the piece is admitted into work regardless of what you planned ahead of time. In this case, clearly, I was working in a period of mourning and the piece is about animate /inanimate states, life/death situations. In retrospect I simply felt my vocabulary had been perhaps unneccesarily limited and why not allow figuration? — it would allow more expression. Had I been as generous as I could be?

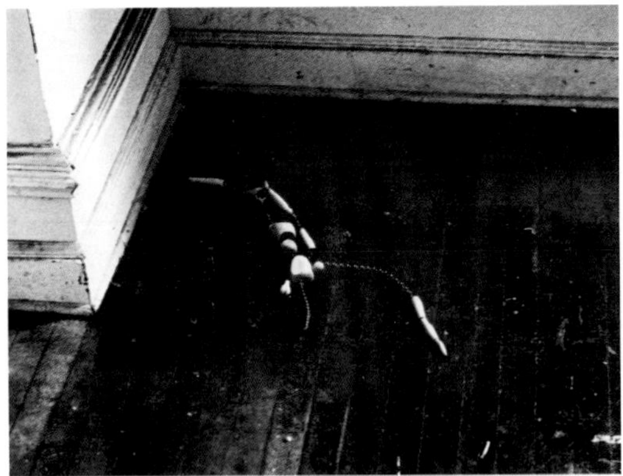

Fig. 5   Untitled, 1974

What's interesting to me in that figure is the one element that's up, the raised leg. It seems to me there is a lot of struggle in it.

Well, to me it is more interesting than that. The entire piece struggles to be there.

Did this change your work?

This piece is still psychologized. Somehow meaning wasn't denied in the work. If anything, it was amplified. It was much easier for people to deal with sentiment — with sentimental notions — than to deal with actually real, present experience. And I think actually a lot of the work that received considerable attention in the late '70s — after '75 —was work that isolated images, and people would react to the images. It's an interesting idea, but I'm not sure how real it was, or how complete the experience was.

In 1974, you made a piece from an artist's mannequin that was later destroyed (Fig. 5). Could you tell something about it? Is there a relationship between the mannequin's wire and wood forms and the wires and blocks in your recent work?

Yes, I guess in a way, there's a relationship. When I did that mannequin piece I was pretty angry, and I was interested in busting up the form, busting up the human form. So I pulled it apart. I think I was using the mannequin as a model. I was frustrated. I had lots of anger and rage and the mannequin seemed an effective place to locate it. I pulled it apart and just threw it around the room. It seemed like a good vehicle, so I just ripped the whole thing apart. It's a pretty aggressive piece.

The comparison that Roberta Smith makes to Giacometti's* Woman with Her Throat Cut *is that something that was conscious, unconscious, or not related at all?

I think a relationship exists. You end up not so much looking at other work, as having a commensurate experience with what one can imagine has inspired another artist — this is quite common and of course there is a common language of form. I think in sculpture there are certain ideas about leaning, certain ideas about verticality, horizontality, that at least in our culture — Western culture — are significant, that absolutely seem to be manifestations of human psychology. I think the formal language also transcends cultures to some extent. It's not so much psychology, as it's — I hate to use the term — thought. The fact is that a particular arrangement of forms becomes the sign, the symbol, of a whole world of thought. And I think there is a commonality in that.

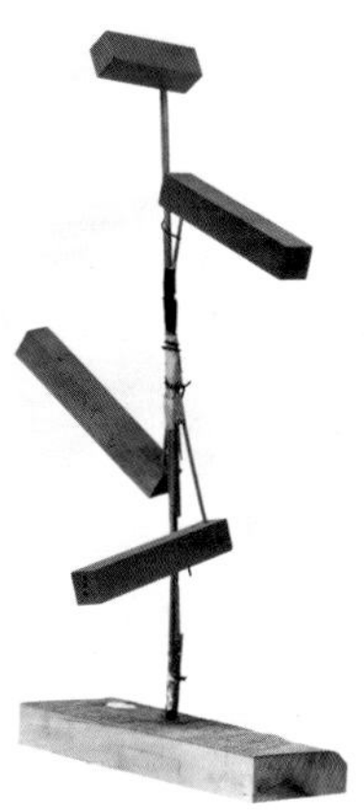

Fig. 6   Untitled, 1988-90

I think you get to a point where your work develops, and it becomes less about idea and more about real experience, and you come up against people who have had similar experiences. If you're a sculptor, the sculptors you admire end up having dealt with similar notions. Somehow the same information is revealed, but it is revealed in a very different context.

So if a comparison is made between that mannequin piece of mine and the Giacometti, it's a legitimate comparison, and I'm sure that the input, and the anger and frustration may have been similar — which is interesting — but the piece is not derived from the Giacometti.

Was I interested in *Woman with Her Throat Cut*? Yes, I've always been interested in that piece. But I mean, you would have to be wouldn't you? If you are a sculptor and interested in the 20th century and that piece doesn't interest you, you would have a serious problem. That's one of the key pieces. The reason why it intrigues me, and would intrigue anybody, it that it seems to embody rage and brutality. Women may not like it. It's all about cutting up, it's very brutal. I think men have to deal with that level of anger that they have against women. Giacometti does makes that confrontation and that's why it's a profoundly important piece, aside from its formal invention.

Does the little model on the floor (Fig. 6) relate to the mannequin?

I tried for years to do that piece where the figure dissolves and departs. How do you deal with that separation of parts, and that explosion of the figure? How do you suspend these things in space? I want them pulled apart, but I want them to relate to each other. In a way that was done in the mannequin piece.

One piece we're going to have in the show (JS 865, Pl. 25) seems to function the same way.

It does to some extent. But the problem in that piece is you still have the shafts. It would be nice to have those relationships without the structure that holds the piece up. One of the interesting and difficult things about making sculpture — in fact the problem one has to overcome — is the physical limits of the material. You're always up against the actual mass, the actual material itself. Its weight, its mass, denies the spirit. You have to overcome that in order to form the piece. Most large sculpture is appalling. One of the problems with a large sculpture is that the material is so difficult. It's so heavy, it's so bulky, it's so hard to join things, that by the time you do something that's large, it's generally dead. In other words, it loses all character, all spirit is denied.

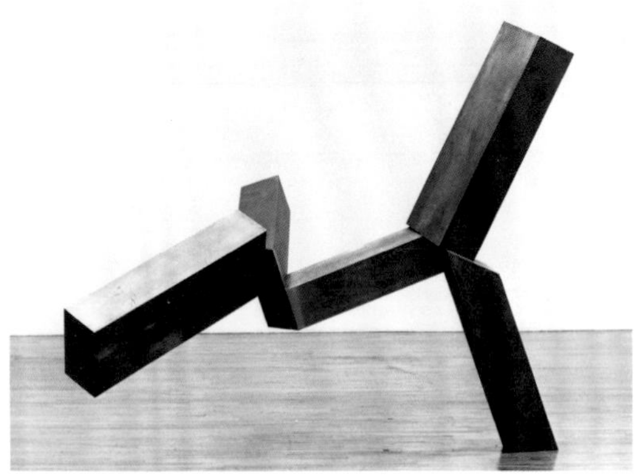

Fig. 7   Untitled, 1989 (JS 867)

I've been fascinated by how your work keeps that spirit.

That's something you have to will. When I was in Paris last fall working on prints I went to the Musee d'Orsay. One interesting aspect of that museum for me is the great collection of Carpeaux. A lot of people dislike Carpeaux. The fact of the matter is, Carpeaux is extremely interesting, because Carpeaux can go from a model to a large piece and still retain the spirit of his discovery, which is a tremendous achievement. How do you retain that life and vitality in work from size to size? It's about strength of intention, it's about staying on top of the work, really. Some pieces I can conceive in their full size, other pieces I can't.

Most of your sculpture does not have any gender.

Well, some of it has gender. It enters into certain pieces. There are specific pieces that you could read as male, that have references to penises. There are certain pieces I think of more as female that have apertures and holes, that deal with female anatomy. They're not that explicit. It's a sign, a metaphor. I think they generally have a gender bias. The piece at Des Moines (JS 735, Pl. 20), for example, is pretty hard not to read as female.

The position?

You'd have to be pretty blind not to pick that up. You read it's horizontality as vulnerable. There is a tenderness in the work that I see as female. By the treatment of the surface, I can accent the piece and pull it toward a certain realm. The same thing happens in another sculpture, the vertical painted wood piece (JS 712, Pl. 18).

When do you decide to do something in wood or cast it in bronze?

Well, at this point since the work's become big, it's become a structural decision. The piece we're looking at now cannot exist in wood (JS 867, Fig. 7). You couldn't work in wood that size without having external supports and braces, a scaffolding.

When something is small enough to be realized in wood, do you prefer wood?

Sometimes. In general, wood doesn't interest me that much. Not any more. I'm much more interested in the insistence of casting.

The presence, the solidity?

No. I will use wood when I want to retain a delicacy, maybe an immediacy. It depends on what presence I want. Wood is fast. You can cut it up and join it together. Great material to realize form. Once

I have the form, I tend to cast in bronze. I'm more interested in the insistence of bronze than the vulnerability of wood.

Please explain the translation of wood into bronze.

Taking something from wood into bronze actually becomes very interesting. I think in certain work it bothered me that the bronze referred to wood so explicitly, that in looking at the bronze you would be reminded of a beam, for example. One way of bypassing the wood is casting plaster into plywood — the piece refers only to the surface that it came from, rather than to another three-dimensional form.

Plaster into plywood into bronze?

Yes. Let's look at this piece (JS 866, Pl. 1). If I want to make that top piece — that chest, that torso — I would first make a wood model. When I have a keen idea of what size I want it to be, I'd make it that size in foamcore because it's easy to do — it's fast. Speed is important so you do not lose sight of your intention. Then I might adjust it. When I'm satisfied, I'd build a plywood box where the internal dimension is the same as the external dimensions of the foamcore model. Then I pour plaster into the plywood form.

The surface of the plaster picks up the surface of the plywood. Plywood has no direction to it. When you look at a piece of plywood — when you build a box out of plywood and you cast inside of it — the textures and patterning don't necessarily correspond to the growth of lumber. So, it doesn't refer back to another extant state of the sculpture. The pieces never existed in wood.

There's no ghost.

There's no memory of another form, whereas the other works had a memory, particularly if they were cast monolithically from lumber. Where all the parts were joined and then a cast was made, the bronze very much referred to another extant state. Now it doesn't. I think that it evolved in the work because the forms became so complicated that they could no longer really be made in wood the size I wanted them to be. Or if they were made in wood, it was such an elaborate ordeal that any interest in the piece would dissipate, on my part. I mean, they were crafted. I have made some wood pieces that were huge, and an absolute pain to make. They are elaborate, made out of plywood construction with joinery — they can end up looking like furniture.

But if I make the plaster from plywood, and then cast the bronze from the plaster, there is enough

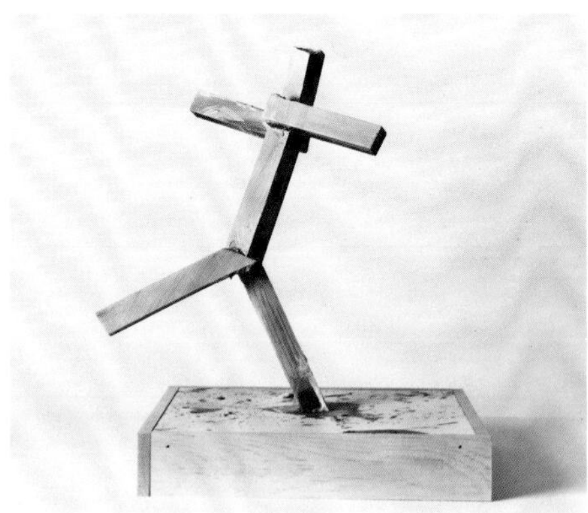

Fig. 8 Untitled, 1989 (JS 889)

play and activity in the making so that the realization of the final piece is not that different from it's initial conception. Now, certain pieces you would join in wood and leave them in wood, because really you want intimacy in the piece. So that would be the answer — an elaborate, round-about answer — to your question.

Have you painted any of the bronze pieces?

I've painted a couple, not a whole lot. For example, one I did this summer, where I was interested in masking the bronze (JS 889, Fig. 8). I have patinated a few pieces. I don't like to patinate programmatically because I think it masks the process. Traditionally there have been two reasons to patinate: one was to unify the surface, cover up defects of workmanship; the other was to make it look ancient. But a bronze develops its own patina over time, and I'd rather have it happen naturally.

What the paint will do is deny the material, the bronze or the wood. It's very conceptual. It's very abstract. Bronze is abstract too. But wood is very physical, organic; it's natural, it's a fact, it's a found material. As soon as you start to paint it, you start to deny it. You start to introduce this much more mental state, more abstract state. So that's always interested me.

The little painted running man piece (JS 167A, Pl. 4) that you did in 1976-77....

I chose to paint it in order to break the form up. It was too stylized. So I thought by painting it I would improve it. The piece was about motion, but it was very rigid. It has taken me a long time to introduce a significant level of movement into my work, and at that point I wasn't quite capable of doing it. I think that the tree, which also deals with movement, is about some life/death situation, very internal (JS 155, Pl. 3), and the figure is about a running away from it, an avoidance of it. The figure was rigid and stiff and formal, and it was much more about received information, much more external. Then I painted it. And I was so terrorized, I didn't know how to paint it. So I literally projected theatrical light on it — and I painted where the shadows fell. The idea was to break the piece up. I was trying to create a metaphor by projecting light on the piece — it's about the relationship of light to the breaking up of form. Using the light was also a formal device to justify, to save the piece.

I think when you work you are aware of the strengths or the weaknesses of what you are doing. If you are ambitious enough, you recognize a piece's weakness and you can strengthen it. You can find some way of strengthening it. I think that level of recognition is important. That's what work is about — that level of analysis — nothing else.

Why do you keep all your works untitled?

I always felt that language would take away from the experience of the piece. I was hesitant to use language, because I wanted the piece to communicate, not the language assigned to it. I guess I have an aversion to language in art. I would rather visually experience art than read art. When language is a surrogate for visual experience I find it boring.

Some of your pieces can be seen as very sad in some respects, but also as very joyous in others. Different people can feel different emotions from the same figure. By leaving the works untitled are you inviting that possibility?

I think that most of my pieces deal with ambivalence. They're upright but collapsing. I think they deal with both modes. I think to some extent, they deny their own presence. If I had a more poetic bent for language I might find titles that were appropriate.

This piece is interesting, with two forms as two heads (JS 391A, Pl. 5). Roberta Smith in her Whitney catalogue essay discussed the motion of such double figures and the alter-ego effect of the heads. Is there any relationship to Futurism in dealing with motion, dealing with energy?

Well, probably not. Futurism is a movement that I've always disliked. Probably what doesn't interest me about Futurism is it's singular direction. Futurism at its worst is about a linear sequence in time. I think that what interested me more than movement in the double headed piece, was the possibility of articulating different but simultaneous states of mind. Again, I had wood which was found, and to make the wood figure I cut and glued pieces together. The wax, though, is modeled, so you develop the form rather than just take the form. I mean, I cut the wood — and I cut say, a 1" x 1" x 5" piece — but cutting it on a tool is very different from developing the form in wax. In wood, the form existed before it was joined, but in wax the form was developed before it existed. That's what interests me, the juxtaposition of the two.

It's not so much a metaphor for an alter-ego as a reference back to the piece. Referring back to the piece, a check on the piece, a counter motion, another state. Believe me when I first did those figures, I was very suspicious: "What is this, is this any good? What have I gotten into?" Then all of a sudden you're casting five pieces, six pieces of wood, joined together, into bronze. The modeling of the piece was a counter to that. A denial of the assertion of the piece. What I'm saying is, you take pieces of wood — the initial figure that I did — you slam them together and you cast the piece. So all of a sudden I've made this figure, this standing sculpture, which was very antithetic to the drift at the time. It was very assertive. The casting into bronze was an insistence on the piece in time.

And it was running against the grain of much of what was going on in the late '70s, early '80s.

I think a little bit. I do think that the overriding demand of 20th-century sculpture — probably art in general—is that it functions in the real world — that it have some grounding in the real world. And that it is relevant. It's not about some glorification of self. It's about some real discovery. It has some real significance. That's why it's not on a pedestal. That's why it's on the floor. So it occupies the space we occupy.

I think one thing that I wanted in my work— even with those pieces that were so psychologized, dealing with intimate personal injury—was that they at least have a ring that was true, in terms of my state of mind at the time. I wanted them to reflect what I was thinking. Actually, the whole movement to larger work occupying real space was an attempt to have things that function in the real world. But they had to be grounded. There are moments when you look at your work and you think: "Well, this is really crap, and it's just fabrication." I think the countering of that is important. The embodiment of it's denial in it's assertion is significant. And that's what that secondary figure might be more about. It's really this analytical situation. Yes, of course, the doubling does give movement. And it gives a reality that might visually correspond more with one's sense of self than looking at a static, two-armed, two-legged, one-headed figure. Seeing those multiple limbs and two heads might be a more accurate depiction of one's sense of being in the world, and there are other pieces where I've used that. There were double heads and double bodies. I'm still using double torsos.

In a piece like this (JS 391A, Pl. 5) that's seen at so many different angles, is Cubism an interest?

I think abstraction is the most interesting idea, and an idea that is far from resolved. Cubism is interesting. Surrealism, Cubism, they're fascinating. I think if you are working in 1990 all of that stuff

is information. It's vocabularly that you can
absorb — it is there to be integrated into the work.
Yes, my work deals with lots of surreal notions
and lots of notions that probably have been touched
on, or worked on, by early 20th-century artists.
The more you fully understand Cubism — probably
the more useful it is

**What do you think about abstraction in
general.**

The idea of thinking, of thought, and the translation
of human experience into form — whether it's
painting or sculpture — is a tremendously abstract
concept. Maybe sculpture is less abstract than
painting because it exists in real space; painting
doesn't.

**What is the relationship of present works to
past works of yours?**

Within your own work you resolve certain problems,
you come to certain conclusions, for a period of
time. Then all of a sudden, eight years later, you're
talking about that mannequin piece in relationship to the recent work. They're close. The impetus
is similar, and I didn't realize that. I didn't think
about it, but clearly I apply 25 years of work — or
what-ever it's been, 20 years of work to each piece.
I think you are always rediscovering things.

Penetrate as far as you're capable of penetrating,
then you feel that you have resolved it, and
really you haven't, and you go back. It's what's fascinating about it, and it's very frustrating too.
And it's like all relationships; you're bound to repeat
the past to some extent, to rediscover and revise.

**Let's talk about this bronze (JS 383A, Pl. 6)
from the early '80s with its striking contraposto
configuration.**

It's a female figure. Actually that piece I worked
from the model.

From a live model?

Yeah, actually there was someone in front of me
when I put the piece together. That's something I
rarely do. I kept thinking that if I was dealing
with a female image, that using a model would be a
viable way of working. I'm familiar with my own
anatomy, the internal feeling of body — kinesthesin
I suppose. But then all of a sudden I have to deal
with a breast. So, I needed someone to stand so I
could look and study and reference. I've done that
only a few other times, very early, when I was
concerned with female figuration. I keep thinking
I'll do it again, when I get in a lull. I could con-
ceivably work with a model, chiefly to understand
organizing the form. But it's tough to get someone

to hang around when you're chopping wood. It's
not like they're sitting there comfortably — what
with dust in their faces.

*Why do you want to display this figure on a
shelf? On the wall?*

Because it is pretty frontal.

*You used a shelf in the earlier work — the
houses of 1973-75?*

I used the shelf as a device to isolate those pieces
from the real space.

*This will be the only work in the exhibition that
is on a plinth. In that sense, it's an anomaly.
It's also a much more traditional-looking image
than your other work. What was the interest
in the contraposto?*

It just seemed like a refrain. I think it was a lighter
moment in the work. There are a couple of
pieces that have breasts, and that were female, and
that I specifically wanted to be female and I felt
they didn't function abstractly on the same level. If
the work is abstract enough I think it gets away
from that male/femaleness.

*The legs in your work are the most expressive
of any of the limbs.*

Do you think so? They anchor the piece. They
make the connection from the piece to the ground,
so they could be seen as being the most animated.

*I was actually thinking about the legs that come
off the ground in JS 595, (Pl. 14).*

Well, fine, but there is always one anchored to the
ground. In the piece you're talking about one leg
is on the ground, while the other kicks and moves.

It's the contrast of the two.....

One holds and the other is expressive. I don't
even think of that stuff when I work, I just do it.
Believe me, all the intellectualizing one does
and all the ways one thinks about the work, and
the critical input, all somehow get subsumed.
When you're working you don't even think about
it. You're just sticking it together.

*The 1980-82 piece with truncated legs (JS 465,
Pl. 7)....*

Where I chopped them down. There was a point
where I wanted a greater sense of necessity. When
you said that the legs were the most expressive, it's
got to do with the angle of attachment — 35 degree,

45 degree, various angles going off into space.
There was a point when there were too many op-
tions, too many choices. I began to cut them
back and started attaching things at right angles, so
they became more fundamental and less baroque.
In that piece, the truncated leg piece, I think I was
trying to deny excess in the work, to reduce it
to its very human element. I just felt that the long
limbs suddenly seemed gratuitous and so I pro-
ceeded to chop. I probably didn't like the piece and
began hacking away at it, which I frequently do.
JS 497 (Pl. 10) is similar. I developed the piece, built
it, looked at it, and then subverted it by sawing away
and removing different elements. I was attempting
to reduce the piece down to its barest language.

***You mentioned attaching things at angles. What
I am attracted to in all of these pieces are these
areas, where they have been cut and where they
come together in a vast array of angles.***

The joinery is important. It's like looking at a detail
of a painting and finding that the detail is character-
istic of the overall picture. You look at a section of
a Turner, say, and observe the level of atomization
and then when you look at the whole painting
you find it's atomized on a grosser scale. Somehow I
think the complexity in that little area reflects the
rest of the complexity. It's not an isolated incident.

Why did you paint JS 466 (Pl. 8)?

You know Picasso's sleeping females, those big
circular Picassos? Women in a dream state? When
I saw them at the Picasso retrospective at The
Museum of Modern Art they intrigued me with the
use of color, particularly the use of violet—that
dreamy color that dissolves edges. Each color has
a perceptual effect, which I was trying to figure
out when I did those geometric wall pieces in '78,
'79. This figure was moving, but on the ground. The
mood of the form was amplified by paint.

There's a tension in the arm and in the leg.

That the painting of the head amplifies.

The dream going on in the head?

I thought of it as an active/dormant figure. It is
the contrast between the violet color and the
physical fact of the piece. The contrast between
paint and wood is very powerful. It's similar to
the contrast between bronze and paint, bronze and
wood, and so on.

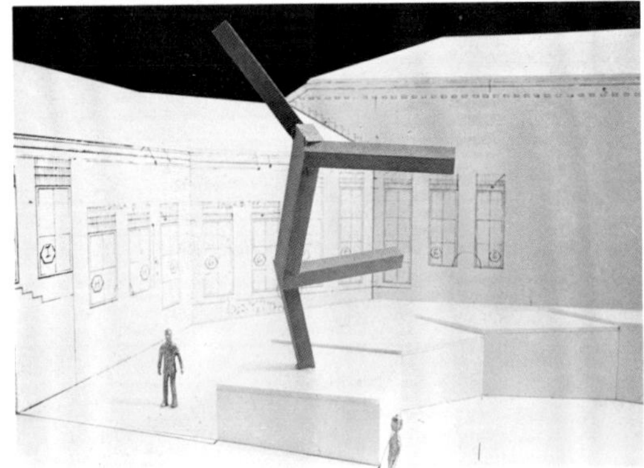

Fig. 9   Untitled, 1990

You're talking about paint dissolving the wooden form.

Yeah, it does.

The next piece is on its head, turning a cart-wheel (JS 467, Pl. 9).

I think that was just another way of subverting the form. I see it as crashing into the ground.

Standing it on it's head?

Yes. The piece I'm working on for the Hood at Dartmouth has more inversion (Fig. 9). I want that piece to invert so that it appears to configure up and down simultaneously, so that arms read as legs and vice versa. It reads more abstract. There's one in the show that does that, JS 595 (Pl. 14).

The Dartmouth commission involves a number of new directions in your work. When are you interested in making a shift?

There's part of you that gets bored with what you're doing. You realize you're just wasting your time. The Dartmouth commission interests me a lot — because of its sheer size. The piece is 21 feet high — that's challenging. I'm dealing with a specific site and architectural situation — a courtyard in a Charles Moore building.

When do you chose to have something unique and when do you make an edition?

That depends to a large extent on how I make the piece. There are two ways of bronze casting. One is basically a variation of the lost wax process — the contemporary version is called ceramic shell. You take a work made of wood and make a rubber mold of the wood, and remove the wood and fill the mold with wax, then remove the wax, and dip the wax in ceramic — the slurry's a liquid — and let it dry, and then pull it out, and make a couple of coats, let it dry, stick the ceramic into an oven, fire it. As the ceramic hardens and vitrifies, the wax melts out. If you do that you can do an edition because you have the rubber mold.

However, another way of doing it is just taking a wood sculpture and dipping it into ceramic slurry itself — skipping the mold — and burning out the wood. So you build ceramic around the wood, then you put that in the oven and the wood burns up, and the ceramic vitrifies and you have a unique piece. This way is a more expedient, direct way of casting. I use it if I want to see the piece quickly. Though, for the most part, to do a unique bronze is silly, because the whole notion of casting an edition is an intrinsic part of working with bronze.

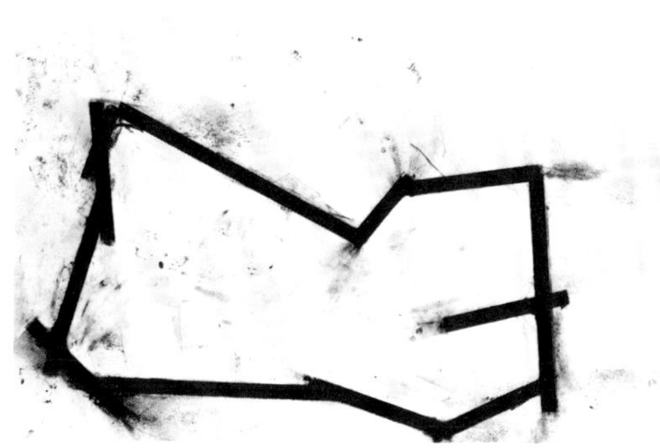

Fig. 10   Untitled, 1981 (JS 435)

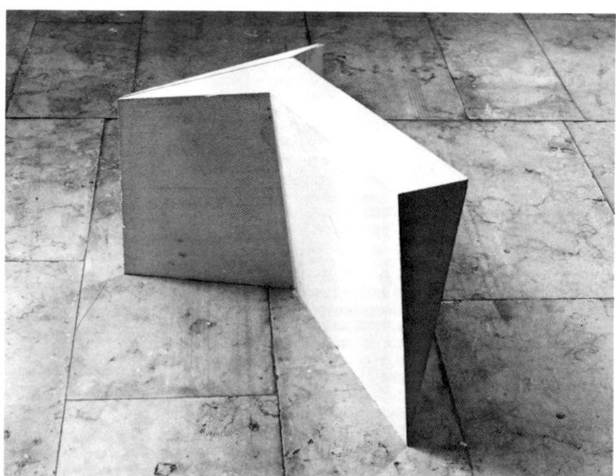

Fig. 11   Untitled, 1981 (JS 455)

The piece that you said you built and then hacked away is headless as well as having truncated legs (JS 467, Pl. 9). When do you use a head on the figures and when do you do without?

I think if you eliminate the head, you focus more on the form. The head becomes so depictive, so descriptive. It can exclude the more abstract reading of the work. I think sometimes you can deal with the headless form more kinesthetically, instead of representationally.

This next figure — talking about gender — seems incredibly male (JS 584, Pl. 11).

You could see that as somebody looking at, contemplating, so to speak, his penis. That's pretty gender specific.

Let's go on to the next piece, the wedge form (JS 587, Pl. 12). Initially, I didn't see it as a figure at all.

Well, I don't think of it as a full figure — I saw it as a torso and a back — more female. I worked on this one from a model. There were a lot of studies — all of those drawings in the Whitney catalogue plus plasters I made in Jerusalem (Figs. 10 and 11).

I saw the piece relating more to your houses....

That wedge has all kinds of references to female form, to the human torso, to architecture, to houses. What I'm trying to say is that I think it's inevitable that work is referential. You would have to set up very severe, rigid conditions in order that work refer only to itself or to the maker's mind at that moment.

But more importantly I think I was interested in the hollowness of the piece, its emptiness. The fact that it is open on both sides, gives you access to the interior of the piece, greater admission, entrance, into the work.

Now, this little crouched figure, all in a ball (JS 593, Pl. 13).

I don't know if that's the best example of that moment, but it was a very critical time in the work. My original idea about working with the crouched figure was that by seeing the small size and the configuration you would think defense. This went back to the early running man sculpture, and the tree sculpture, and there was a group of three pieces on the floor that L.A. County owns that were done

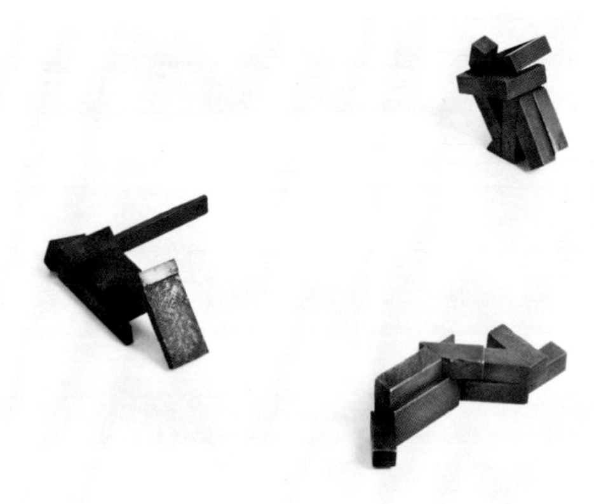

Fig. 12   Untitled, 1980 (JS 358A,B,C)

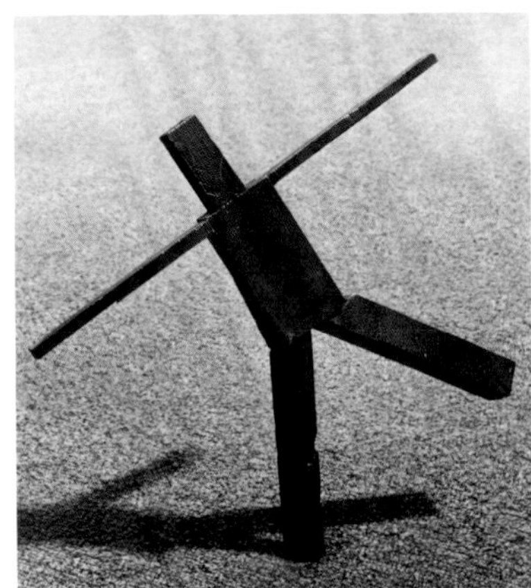

Fig. 13   Untitled, 1980 (JS 357)

in maybe 1980 (Fig. 12), that consisted of three small figures: one was this sort of defended figure like the crouch piece; a second was a sort of sleeping figure; and the third was a female form with breasts, lying on its back. They were pretty bulky and very small, about six or seven inches high. The posture of the pieces would key your reading.

So if you look at this little crouch piece (JS 593, Pl. 13), this explicit image, "boom," you have an idea of what it means, without having to really, fully experience the piece physically in your space. It's like a quick take. It's like reading.

I found that was fine as long as you're dealing with depressed, dormant poses, but as soon as I began to deal with more elated states I realized I had to do them larger. The first standing figure, this little tiny figure on one leg, arms sticking out (JS 357, Fig. 13), all of a sudden that elation seemed precious in that size. It had to be really large. And that's when I began to work full size. It was a real moment in my work. You know — a pivotal moment.

What caused the change between the more defensive to the more elated?

My mood. I could not stand dealing with the magical world of that early work. All those houses, and defended bunkers. As beautiful as that work may appear, it was quite tortured. I began to feel that I could introduce an element of joy into the work without feeling ridiculous.

That piece (JS 595, Pl. 14) seems so like dance.

I am interested in movement, in dislocation of mass. I am interested in dance, in the way I'm interested in sports. I'm interested in the dislocation of the body from the ground.

That piece has a feeling of celebration.

The piece is very interesting to me because it is a mirror image. There's a doubling, an inversion of the same form. You have two torsos — two masses that come together and compress, and you have those linear elements reaching out, one stabilized and the other three reaching out. It really becomes quite dynamic and has a lot to do with movement. In order to lift one leg you have to support different mass on the other leg. There's a lot of reaching and coming together.

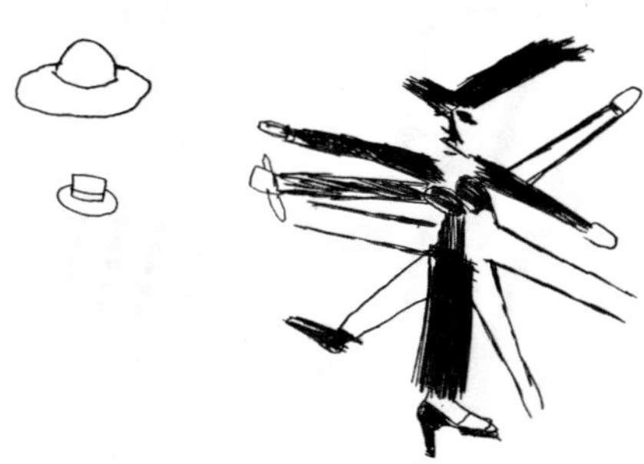

Fig. 14   Untitled, 1975 (JS 142C, detail)

A lot of circular movement. There's one 1975 print of fighting couples in which the couples are shown in a circle together (Fig. 14). Is that sort of the same?

I don't think so. I guess there are certain pieces that are more static and more introverted. And the piece we're talking about now is very expansive. I didn't answer your question. What was the question?

It was about the fighting couples.

I don't know! I think you look for possible ways of engagement. Fighting is a primitive means of engagement — an argument or a fight, particularly between couples or friends. I'm not talking about physical fighting, but discourse. It's not the most rational discourse, but it's active, it's a method of resolution. It is much better than remaining passive. To answer your question there is no relationship between this piece and the image of the fighting couple.

But I do think that the notion of using anger as a channel for work is an interesting idea. When you're working you utilize every means of finding form or expressiveness. Anger is a vital emotion. I think you try to channel it into work. I don't think it is the highest level. You have to get through that, you have to deal with that to get on to everything.

Talking about the next piece from 1985 (JS 612, Pl. 15), with that open head....

I think what it does is pull you inside of work. Instead of being stopped at the surface of the work, you have access inside the piece. You see its hollowness, you see its artifice.

We talked about that while discussing the wedge piece (JS 587, Pl. 12).

Yes, but in the wedge you have no illusion that the piece is solid. It reveals itself immediately as a passageway or tunnel. However, in this piece that appears to be solid and is then revealed to be hollow, the access afforded by disclosure actually is a kind of debunking. And in the debunking of the piece, the revelation of its artifice, it becomes even more emotionally available — vulnerable. It has a humility to it that not all my work has.

Have you ever had any interest in Cycladic figures?

No. I was interested in the frontality of Egyptian work, and very interested in Southeast Asian art. I was in India for two years after college, and I looked at a lot of sculpture and a lot of architecture. What probably interested me the most was Mamallapuram, which is an 8th- or 7th-century temple site outside of Madras. You see these temples with sculpture cut into stone and certain areas where the stone hadn't been cut, where they had just begun and backed off, leaving the beginning of an image emerging out of rock. The sculptor dealing with obdurate material in the 7th century, on the Bay of Bengal in India comes across a very similar situation to what Michelangelo encounters in the Renaissance. They would have had parallel experiences.

Certain physical and psychological states are inevitable considering the confrontation of human and mass. Maybe that's too dramatic. I was trying to get to a point. In the Ajanta/Ellura caves, outside of Aurangabad, there are stone cut temples that start with Brahmanism, then became Buddhist; then Hindu; and then Jain. They start at the 3rd century and end up in the 17th century. And you get this tremendous sense of progress and process. Within each moment there is elevation, depression, celebration, and reserve. To sense this continuity — to see this huge unfolding — was really a profound experience. It wasn't studying Indian art so much as it was seeing the development of an idea from its beginning to its conclusion in some kind of chronological sequence, which is something that's is

perhaps not available in your own culture because you're too busy trying to locate yourself in it. Frequently you need a kind of external forum. It's hard to step outside, and what are you going to look at here, at least in terms of sculpture? Carved women on the front of ships? So all of a sudden you go to India, you go to Southeast Asia, and you see a whole world revealed.

This next piece (JS 624, Pl. 16) is going to be in Des Moines for the show, and another (JS 625, Pl. 17), which is owned by Baltimore, is going to be shown when the exhibition travels there.

Similar pieces; one's larger and one's smaller.

The Baltimore piece is bigger?

It's not that different in configuration from this piece (JS 595, Pl. 14). The difference is that JS 624 (Pl. 16) is being supported without a device. It's tripodal, resting on its own weight, instead of having some mechanical device holding it up. Again, there's less illusion in the piece — the piece rests on its own, the way we rest. But we have big feet, so they kind of hold us down. The other piece (JS 595, Pl. 14) is bolted to the ground, its projection of movement is an illusion. They have the same figurative elements; two torsos and a bunch of limbs.

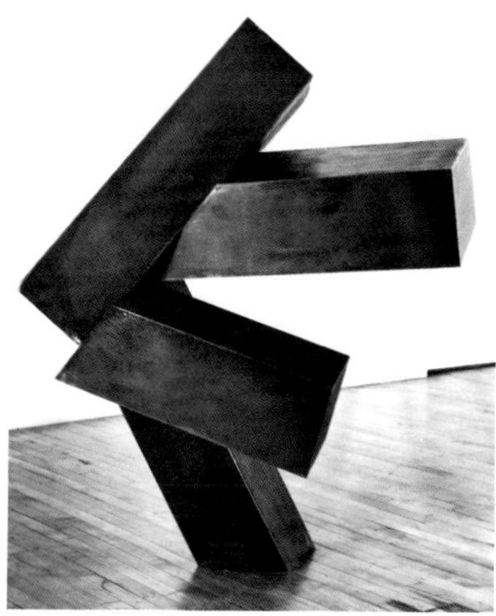

Fig. 15   Untitled, 1989-90 (JS 893)

Suddenly there was a point where I was tired of bolting stuff to the ground — it just seemed to me too baroque, too 19th-century — and I just wanted to rest. So that was a reaction. Let the piece find its own place.

This painted wood piece (JS 712, Pl.18) is one you described earlier as possessing a female quality — a certain tenderness.

In that piece I wanted a very simple, reduced gesture. I was playing with two legs and I found a relationship that really corresponded to what I was looking for. I put them on the ground and it just required a torso. It had this very subtle movement — just what I wanted. This torso was made from fleshy, pink fir, very open grained, a kind of tough, crude country wood, from a saw-mill. I wanted to unify the two pieces of wood, but the wood was so woody, it had so much wood quality — various knots here and there, cracks. I felt that a slight amount of pigment, of white paint, would create a veil around the piece and envelop it. It would pull you away from the woodiness so you could deal with it more in terms of figuration, and in terms of my intentions.

The joining of the torso to those legs is critical.

It's very critical. Basically you take two limbs which when joined together set up a plane. I work with very severe limitations. I do model, but with quite a reduced vocabulary. I'm hesitant to introduce anything new into the vocabulary unless I find it necessary. So, I will try with the least amount of parts to express the most that I can. The legs, of course, create plane; it's that plane that determines the possible arrangements. The whole relationship of the torso to the legs in JS 893 (Fig. 15) is radically different. That is a departure. I mean, all these things seem so minor but in fact they're significant. Unfortunately.

Why unfortunately?

I mean I would like to be more fluid. It is very hard to synthesize a thought into form. You establish a working vocabulary you feel comfortable with. And I think it's those times when you're reaching, when you're extending your ideas into the material itself, that you realize what you can do. Those are the exciting moments. Not having retrospectives. And I'm serious about that. Those are the moments you really work for — I'm sure the one moment where you can recognize what you could never do before, where you synthesize and transcend past

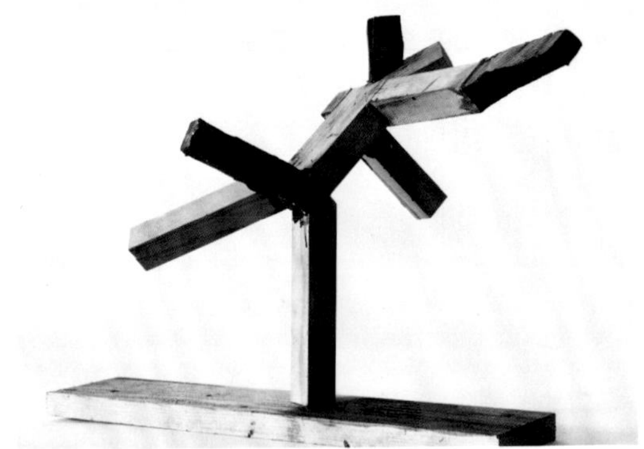

Fig. 16   Untitled, 1980-81 (JS 391)

knowledge. It's this capacity to recognize that you can do something that was out of your reach before. That's really exhilarating. You know when it's a good piece. So when I flopped that torso (JS 893, Fig. 15) down I knew that was a moment of resolution.

When you achieve that kind of major accomplishment it opens a whole lot of possibilities, I assume.

I think it does, but it unfolds slowly, not all of a sudden. Every piece that I do is a serious struggle — it's hard. And I tell you, it gets harder and harder. The more I know, the higher my standards are. The more I've experienced from my work, the more I want to experience from my work, and it becomes tough. You look at a piece, and it's not good enough. In my last show I had three pieces, four pieces, and they were all interesting pieces. And that's what I want. I don't want anything less.

I think artists actually get better as they get older. Art is one of the few fields in which that's true. But then, I think as you work, as you get older, your work becomes less radical. Subversiveness is no longer such an issue. You have basically established the vocabulary. That's when it becomes more and more difficult, because your standards are higher.

Well, if you keep producing, you have to continually challenge yourself.

I think that's what happens. And it becomes a little slow. I spent the last three or four years doing kind of significant pieces, where I really did a lot of reaching. And now it's slowed down a little bit. But that commission for Dartmouth, that's exciting — the scale, the size, and the kind of freedom of joining the piece, the immediacy of it is exciting (Fig. 9). And now if I can translate that immediacy into larger size, it's quite exhilarating.

What else interests you now?

I've always been interested in some combination of modeling and the immediacy of additive work. We were talking about that in that little figure made with wax and wood (JS 391, Fig 16); now that it's cast in bronze (JS 391A, Pl. 5) you still sense it. I did it on a larger scale, that piece. It was very effective.

There are lots of ideas that interest me. Purely abstract work interests me, where it's less referential, but pregnant and meaningful. That house that I always thought of as a head — those pieces interest me a lot. There is a lot that I haven't fully explored. To some extent female imagery interests me more, abstraction interests me more. And that model (Fig. 6) where those blocks are

suspended. How can you take five chunks of wood
and organize them in a significant way and avoid
figuration? If I can find a way of working in space,
in loading things up with meaning that transcends
figuration, that would be interesting to do.

Does your work relate to David Smith's in that respect?

I probably admire the body of David Smith's work
more than individual pieces. I think he's a great
sculptor. There's a human struggle that exists in
David Smith's work that affects the arrangement of
the forms. That's what interests me in the work.
Now, whether David Smith's work is fully abstract
or not isn't quite the issue. There is a kind of
anthropomorphism and human quality, humanity,
that informs the work, that informs the organization
of forms. If you're next to a David Smith you can
sense the artist. You can sense the maker. I have
the same sense with certain Calders, because of the
strength of the line, you have the sense of the
playfulness of the mind behind it. That aspect of
the work interests me much more than figuration.
I'm not interested in compartmentalization, where
the work occurs outside of one's experience.

Mathematical?

It is not a question of mathematical analysis. I am
talking about where the meaning of the work
is posited outside of the work itself — where the
genesis of the work is external. I'm really interested
in the invention and not sacrificing — not so much
the human condition as the internality of work.
The internality of work interests me much more
than some sort of program, design or theory.

Let's move on to this piece (JS 720, Pl. 19), with its multiple, strange components.

The enigmatic piece. I like that piece a lot. That
piece isn't so explicit. It's very complicated.
It's about torsos, heads, lines of connection, lines
as metaphors, supports that become metaphors for
thought. I can't articulate what that work is about.
It's an introduction of new supports. That piece was
really a reaching out into unknown areas.

Did the thinning of those forms lead to your use of these shafts in JS 790 (Pl. 23)?

No. Go back to the wedge piece we spoke about
(JS 587, Pl. 12). It seemed that as long as things
rested on the ground they had to refer to architecture — if they were abstract forms, that is. If
they were figurative, they had limbs, so you could

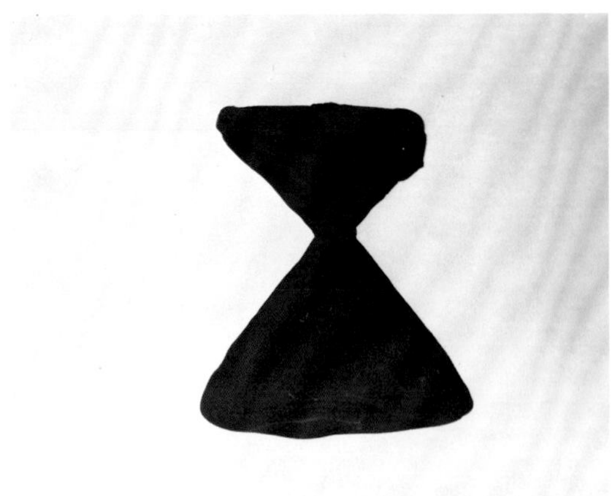

Fig. 17   Untitled, 1979 (JS 320)

get them up in the air. If they were more abstract, which I was interested in, and sat on the ground, then somehow the perception of the piece was always limited by the architecture it was in. So I began to use sticks of wood to dislocate the mass into the air.

Get it up off the ground.

Get it up off the ground, and then the piece would really function independent of architecture. A square form on the bias would still have its geometry, but it would not be parallel to the wall, and so would be differentiated from it. Another way to achieving that was to toss it up in the air. And that has a lot to do with JS 790 (Pl. 23), with those three sticks. So do I think those sticks are surrogates for limbs? Not necessarily. I was interested in the animation of mass and somehow had to throw it up in the air.

It was about this very complicated spatial arrangement. I can't fully articulate it. If there was a linguistic equivalent I wouldn't do the work. Language is never as concise as art, it's always interpretive. So the form has a significance that language doesn't have. You can use language to describe it, but it's not going to be monosyllabic. And art is almost monosyllabic, or if it's complicated,the syntax is different.

The next piece is the big striding figure (JS 767, Pl. 22).

I worked on that piece for years. I wanted a piece that moved both backward and forward simultaneously. So, I ended up cutting the torso and reversing it.

It creates very different postures each way.

Yeah. They bypass each other.

What about the piece whose form looks like a dressmaker's mannequin (JS 793, Pl. 24).

It's an image I've always used in drawing (Fig. 17). The hourglass shape. The armature is a double tetrahedron. I chose that structure because it seemed to imply female figuration. The abruptness of joining wood together was not a viable or evocative method. I chose to model the piece in plaster. I modeled it until the form was full. The shaft removes it from the architecture of the room.

*What about Giacometti's pieces, the vertical,
tall, emaciated, modeled figures?*

Giacometti is one of the great 20th-century
sculptors. But the modeling in this piece is more
like Rodin than Giacometti. The gestures are
larger. Giacometti's are done with his fingers, and
this is done with a hand. It's bigger — the gesture,
the scale is bigger. It has big, aggressive gestures
which are more like Rodin's. With Giacometti, you
have a large incident of gesture effecting a small
mass. This makes the sculpture very active in space.
My piece activates space in a different way. I think
a lot of it has to do with the pinched form, the
way the masses of space on both sides of the piece
pinch the form.

*This piece (JS 865, Pl. 25) is ten feet high.
Obviously it's an open form and you look up
into it. Does it have the same kind of internality of some of the other pieces you discussed?*

Well, it's different. It's a piece that I don't fully
understand. It's open, it's very beautiful and
very delicate. This bronze (JS 866, Pl. 1) is a great
piece. These pieces are big, big scale. I like them.
They're robust, you can't refute them. Deeply
active. Quite full of celebration. Very abstract. I
love that piece. It's my favorite piece.

What about this model for JS 909 (Pl. 26)?

This piece is also exciting. What's interesting about
it is its size. The size is colossal but the sculpture
is made up of two stacked torsos so you can relate
to each section independently. One element
is ascending from the other. I like it. There are
definitely two parts that make up one whole. I
think it's made up of two units we can understand,
that aren't larger than life.

Biography

Born

New York, 1941

Education

New York University, B.A. 1964, M.A. 1969

Awards

National Endowment for the Arts, 1975
Brandeis Award, 1984
Skowhegan Medal for Sculpture, 1986
Award of Merit Medal, 1990 American Academy
   of Arts and Letters

Selected One-Man Exhibitions

1970

Paula Cooper Gallery, New York

1972

Paula Cooper Gallery, New York

1973

The Clocktower, Institute for Art and
   Urban Resources, New York

1974

Paula Cooper Gallery, New York
Galeria Salvatore Ala, Milan

1975

The Garage, London (with Jennifer Bartlett)
Walter Kelley Gallery, Chicago
Paula Cooper Gallery, New York

1976

Paula Cooper Gallery, Los Angeles
Museum of Contemporary Art, Chicago

1977

Max Protetch Gallery, Washington, D.C.
Albright-Knox Art Gallery, Buffalo
Susanne Hilberry Gallery, Birmingham, Michigan
Paula Cooper Gallery, New York
Galerie Gillespie-de Laage, Paris
Galerie Aronowitsch, Stockholm

1978

The Greenberg Gallery, St. Louis
Galerie m, Bochum, West Germany

1979

Akron Art Institute, Akron, Ohio
Paula Cooper Gallery, New York
Galerie Gillespie-de Laage, Paris
Ohio State University, Columbus

1980

The Whitechapel Art Gallery, London (travelled to
  Museum Haus Lange, Krefeld, West Germany
  and Moderna Museet, Stockholm)
Galerie Mukai, Tokyo
Asher/Faure, Los Angeles
Brooke Alexander Gallery, New York (prints)
Delahunty Gallery, Dallas (prints)
Paula Cooper Gallery, New York
Bell Gallery, Brown University, Providence, Rhode
  Island (travelled to Georgia State University,
  Atlanta and The Contemporary Arts Center,
  Cincinnati)

1981

Ackland Art Museum, University of North Carolina,
  Chapel Hill
John Stoller Gallery, Minneapolis
Daniel Weinberg Gallery, San Francisco
The Israel Museum, Jerusalem
Galerie Mukai, Tokyo
Young-Hoffman Gallery, Chicago

1982

Paula Cooper Gallery, New York (drawing)
Portland Center for the Visual Arts, Portland,
  Oregon
Susanne Hillberry Gallery, Birmingham, Michigan
Yarlow/Salzman Gallery, Toronto
Whitney Museum of American Art, New York
  (travelled to Dallas Museum of Fine Arts, Art
Gallery of Ontario, Toronto, La Jolla Museum of
  Contemporary Art)

1983

Galerie Aronowitsch, Stockholm
Paula Cooper Gallery, New York Asher/Faure,
  Los Angeles

1984

Paula Cooper Gallery, New York (drawings)
Galerie Aronowitsch, Stockholm
Paula Cooper Gallery, New York

1985

Knoedler Kasmin, London
Stedelijk Museum Amsterdam (travelled to
  Kunstmuseum Dusseldorf and Staatliche
  Kunsthalle Baden-Baden)

1986

Seattle Art Museum, Seattle, Washington
Galerie Daniel Templon, Paris
The John and Mable Ringling Museum of Art,
  Sarasota, Florida
Paula Cooper Gallery, New York

1987

John Berggruen Gallery, San Francisco
Joel Shapiro: Painted Wood, Hirshhorn Museum
  and Sculpture Garden, Washington, D. C.

1988

Paula Cooper Gallery, New York
Gallery Mukai, Tokyo
Joel Shapiro: Recent Sculptures and Drawings,
  Cleveland Museum of Art

1989

Paula Cooper Gallery, New York
Waddington Gallery, London

1990

Museet i Varberg, Sweden

Selected Group Exhibitions

1969

Anti-Illusion: Procedure/Material, Whitney Museum of American Art, New York
Drawings, Paula Cooper Gallery, New York
Hanging/Leaning, The Emily Lowe Gallery, Hofstra University, Hempstead, New York
Sculptural Annual, Whitney Museum of American Art, New York

1972

Small Series, Paula Cooper Gallery, New York

1973

American Drawings 1963 - 73, Whitney Museum of American Art, New York
New American Graphic Art, Goff Art Museum, Harvard University, Cambridge, Massachusetts

1974

A-Z (with Joe Zucker, Richard Arschwater), 410 West Broadway, New York
71st American Exhibition, the Art Institute of Chicago

1975

Painting, Drawing and Sculpture of the '60's and '70's from the Dorothy and Herbert Vogel Collection, Institute of Contemporary Art, University of Pennsylvania, Philadelphia; The Contemporary Arts Center, Cincinnati
Collectors of the Seventies, Part III, Milton Brutten and Helen Herrick, The Clocktower, The Institute for Art and Urban Resources, New York
34th Annual Exhibition, The Society for Contemporary Art, The Art Institute of Chicago

1976

Scale, Fine Arts Building, New York
Critical Perspectives in American Art, Fine Arts Center Gallery, University of Massachusetts, Amherst
Roelof Louw, Marvin Torfield, Joel Shapiro: New Sculpture, Plans and Projects (Organized by Rosalind Krauss), Fine Arts Building, New York

International Tendencies 1971-1976, Venice Biennale
Critical Perspectives in American Art, The American Pavilion, Venice Biennale
Soho, Akademie der Kunste, West Berlin
Biennale of Sydney, Art Gallery of New South Wales, North Sidney, Australia

1977

1977 Biennial Exhibition, Whitney Museum of American Art, New York
Ideas in Sculpture 1965-1977, The Renaissance Society at the University of Chicago
Documenta 6, Kassel, West Germany
Ten Years: A View of a Decade, Museum of Contemporary Art, Chicago
Scale and Environment: 10 Sculptors, Walker Art Center, Minneapolis
Foire Internationale d'Art Contemporain, Grand Palais, Paris
Early Work by Five Contemporary Artists, The New Museum of Contemporary Art, New York

1978

Jenney, Nauman, Serra, Shapiro, Blum Helman Gallery, New York
Hunt, Jenney, Lane, Rothenberg, Shapiro, Vassar College Art Gallery, Poughkeepsie, New York
Made by Sculptors, Stedelijk Museum, Amsterdam
Dwellings, Neuberger Museum, College at Purchase, State University of New York, Purchase

1979

Whitney Biennial, Whitney Museum of American Art, New York
The Minimal Tradition, Aldrich Museum of Contemporary Art, Ridgefield, Connecticut
Contemporary Sculpture: Selections from the Collection of the Museum of Modern Art, Museum of Modern Art, New York
Decade in Review, Whitney Museum of American Art, New York

1980

Painting in Relief, Whitney Museum of American
Art, New York
Zeitgenossische Plastik, Kulturhistorisches Museum,
Bielefeld, West Germany
Pier + Ocean, Hayward Gallery, London and
Rijksmuseum Kröller-Müller, Otterlo
*Reliefs, Formprobleme Zwischen Skulptur Malerei
und Skulptur im 20 Jahrhundert*, Westfalisches
Landesmuseum, Munster
Drawings: The Pluralist Decade, American
Pavilion, Venice Biennale, Venice
Skulptur im 20. Jahrhundert, Wenkenpark,
Riehen/Basel
American Drawing in Black and White, Brooklyn
Museum, Brooklyn, New York
Nature du Dessin, Centre Pompidou, Paris

1981

Whitney Biennial, Whitney Museum of American
Art, New York
*Constructivism and the Geometric Tradition:
Selections from the McCrory Corporation
Collection*, Detroit Institute of the Arts
Amerkanische Zeichnungen der Siebziger Jahre,
traveling exhibition: Louisiana Museum of
Modern Art, Humlebaek,   Denmark, Kunsthalle
Basel, Stadtische Galerie im Lenbachhause,
Munich, Wilhelm-Hack-Museum,
Ludwigshafen, West Germany

1982

American Prints: 1960 - 1980, Milwaukee Art
Museum, Milwaukee, Wisconsin
Great Big Drawings, Hayden Gallery,
Massachusetts Institutue of Technology,
Cambridge
'Abstraction' et Investissement Libidinal, Galerie
Jolliet, Montreal
*Abstract Drawings 1911 - 1981: Selections from the
Permanent Collection*, Whitney Museum of
American Art, New York
74th American Exhibition, The Art Institute of
Chicago

*Drawings from the Collection of Agnes Gund
Saalfield*, Contemporary Arts Center, Cincinnati
Prints by Contemporary Sculptors, Yale University
Art Gallery, New Haven, Connecticut
*Une Experience Museographique: Echange Entre
Artistes 1931-1982 Pologne - U.S.A.*, A.R.C.
Musée d'Art Moderne de la Ville de Paris
Nature du Dessin, traveling exhibition: Musée
d'Evreux, Musée de Besancon, Maison de la
Culture d'Amiens, Musée de Martigues, Musée
de Rennes, Musée de Perpignan, Salles d'Art
Graphique du M.N.A.M.
Amerikanische Zeichnungen, Galerie Bie derman,
Munich
Body Language, Hayden Gallery, Massachusetts
Institute of Technology, Cambridge
postMINIMALISM, Aldrich Museum of
Contemporary Art, Ridgefield, Connecticut
Correspoondencias: 5 Arquitectos, 5 Escultores,
Palacio de las Alhajas, Madrid (travelled to
Malaga, Bilbao)

1983

Twentieth Century Sculpture: Statements of Form,
Whitney Museum of American Art at Philip
Morris, New York
Back to the USA, Rheinisches Landesmuseum
Bonn (travelled to Kunstmuseum Luzern,
Wurttembergischer Kunstverein Stuttgart)
Moderna Museet 1958 - 1983, Moderna Museet,
Stockholm
*Minimalism to Expressionism: Painting and
Sculpture Since 1965 from the Permanent
Collection*, Whitney Museum of American Art,
New York
ARS 83: Helsinki, The Art Museum of the
Ateneum, Helsinki
Sculpture: The Tradition in Steel, Nassau County
Museum of Fine Art, Roslyn Harbor, New York
New Art, The Tate Gallery, London
The American Artist as Printmaker, Twenty-Third
National Print Exhibition, Brooklyn Museum,
New York

*The First Show: Painting and Sculpture from Eight
Collections 1940 - 1980*, The Museum of
Contemporary Art, Los Angeles
Sculpture on a Small Scale, Galerie Maeght-Lelong,
New York

1984

Drawings 1974 - 1984, Hirshhorn Museum and
Sculpture Garden, Smithsonian Institution,
Washington, D.C.
*American Art Since 1970: Painting, Sculpture, and
Drawings from the Collection of the Whitney
Museum of American Art*, Whitney Museum of
American Art, New York
ROSC '84, The Guinness Hop Store, Dublin, Ireland
American Bronze Sculpture: 1850 to the Present,
The Newark Museum, New Jersey
*Highlights: Selections from the BankAmerica
Corporation Art Collections*, Plaza Gallery,
Concourse Gallery, A.P. Gianni Gallery,
San Francisco
American Sculpture: Three Decades, The Seattle
Art Museum, Washington

1985

Affiliations: Recent Sculpture and Its Antecedents,
Whitney Museum of American Art, Fairfield
County, Connecticut
Imagenes en Cajas, Museo Rufino Tamayo,
Mexico City
*Exhibition-Dialogue on Contemporary Art in
Europe*, Modern Art Center, Calouste
Gulbenkian Foundation, Lisbon
Transformations in Sculpture, The Solomon R.
Guggenheim Museum, New York
Sculpture, Larry Gagosian Gallery, New York
*Contemporary Works from the Collection of the
Museum of Modern Art*, Museum of Modern Art,
New York

1986

*An American Renaissance: Painting and Sculpture
since 1940.* Museum of Art, Fort Lauderdale

Spectrum: The Generic Figure, The Corcoran
Gallery of Art, Washington, D.C.
*Between Geometry and Gesture: American
Sculpture 1965 - 1975*, Palacio de Velazquez, Madrid
The Barry Lowen Collection, The Museum of
Contemporary Art, Los Angeles
Prospect 86, Frankfurter Kunstverein, Shirn
Kunsthalle Frankfurt
*Individuals: A Selected History of Contemporary
Art 1945 - 1986*, The Museum of Contemporary
Art, Los Angeles
*A Century of Modern Sculpture: The Patsy and
Raymond Nasher Collection*, Dallas Museum of
Art; travelled to The National Gallery of Art,
Washington, D.C.
The 4th Japan Ushimado International Art Festival,
Ushimado, Japan
Drawings from the Eighties, Carnegie Mellon
University Art Gallery, Pittsburgh

1988

Big Little Sculpture, Williams College Museum of
Art, Williamstown, Massachusetts
New Art on Paper, The Philadelphia Museum of Art
*Philip Guston, Joel Shapiro, Leon Golub, Sigmar
Polke*, The Saatchi Collection, London
Innovations in Sculpture, The Aldrich Museum,
Ridgefield, Connecticut

1989

No Man's Land/Oen Limitation, Kunsthalle,
Recklinghausen, West Germany
1989 Biennial Exhibition, Whitney Museum
of American Art
La Triennal de dibuix Joan Miro, Fundacio
Joan Miro, Barcelona
Master Drawings 1859 - 1989, Janie C. Lee
Master Drawings, New York

1990

*The New Sculpture 1965 - 75: Between Geometry
and Gesture*, Whitney Museum of American Art,
New York

Selected Bibliography

New York, Whitney Museum of American Art, *Anti-Illusion*, 1969, Essay by Marcia Tucker.

Gilbert-Rolfe, Jeremy, "Joel Shapiro: Works in Progress," *Artforum* (December 1973) pp. 73-74, illus.

Bear, Liza, "Joel Shapiro Torquing, A Dialogue with Liza Bear," *Avalanche*, #11 (Summer 1975), pp. 15-19, illus.

Schwartz, Sanford, "Little Big Sculpture," *Art in America*, #64 (April 1976) pp. 53-55.

Amherst, Fine Arts Center Gallery, University of Massachusetts, *Critical Perspectives in American Art*, April 10 - May 9, 1976. Essay by Rosalind Krauss.

Chicago, Museum of Contemporary Art, *Joel Shapiro*, September 11 - November 7, 1976. Essay by Rosalind Krauss.

Kassel. *Documenta 6*, June - October 1977. Essays by Reinhold Hohl and Manfred Schneckenburger.

New York, Artists Space, Committee for the Visual Arts, *Pictures*, September 24 - October 29, 1977. Essay by Douglas Crimp.

New York, The New Museum of Contemporary Art, *Early Work by Five Contemporary Artists*, November 11 - December 30, 1977. Essay by Marcia Tucker. Interview with the artist by Susan Logan, illus.

Ratcliff, Carter, "Joel Shapiro's Drawings," *The Print Collectors Newsletter*, Vol. IX, #1 (March - April 1978), pp. 1-4, illus.

Field, Marc, "On Joel Shapiro's Sculptures and Drawings," *Artforum*, #16 (Summer 1978), pp. 31-37, illus.

Coplans, John, "Joel Shapiro: An Interview," *Dialogue*, Akron Art Institutue (January/ February 1979), pp. 7-9, illus.

Amsterdam, The Stedelijk Museum, *Made by Sculptors*, 1979.

Riehen/Basel, Wenkenpark, *Skulptur im 20 Jahrhundert*, 1980. Essay by Dr. Reinhold Hohl.

London, Whitechapel Art Gallery, *Joel Shapiro: Sculpture and Drawing*, 1980. Essay by Roberta Smith.

Providence, Rhode Island, Brown University, Bell Gallery. *Joel Shapiro*, 1981. Essay by William Jordy.

Munich, Prestel-Verlag, *Amerikanische Zeichnungen Der Siebziger Jahre*, 1981. Essays by Richard Armstrong, Alfred Kren, Carter Ratcliff, Peter Schjeldahl. Also published in English.

Schwartz, Sanford, "Little Big Sculpture," *The Art Presence*, New York: Horizon Press, 1982, pp. 72-76.

New York, Whitney Museum of American Art, *Joel Shapiro*, October 21, 1982 - January 2, 1983. Essays by Richard Marshall and Roberta Smith.

"The World of Joel Shapiro," *Axis* (Japan) (October 1982), pp. 64-67, illus.

Wolff, Theodore F., "Is Modernism Dead? No, But Maybe Too Ingrown," *The Christian Science Monitor*, November 9, 1982, p. 19, illus.

Jordy, William, "The Sculpture of Joel Shapiro," *The New Criterion*, Vol. 1, #4 (December 1982), pp. 54-57.

Kuspit, Donald, "Manifest Densities," *Art in America*, May 1983, pp. 148-152, illus.

Giminez, Carmen and Munoz, Juan. *Correspondencias: 5 Arquitectos, 5 Escultores*. Madrid: MENSA, 1952.

Los Angeles, Museum of Contemporary Art, *The First Show: Painting and Sculpture from Eight Collections 1940 - 1980*. 1983. Foreword by Julia Brown, essay by Pontus Hulten.

Knight, Christopher. "Joel Shapiro is a Master of 'Monumental' Intimacy." *Los Angeles Herald Examiner*, December 11, 1983, illus.

Washington, D.C., Hirshhorn Museum and Sculpture Garden, Smithsonian Institution, *Drawings 1974 - 1984*, March 15 - May 13, 1984. Essay by Frank Gettings.

Berger, Maurice, "Joel Shapiro: War Games," *Re-Dact: An Anthology of Art Criticism*, No. 1, 1984, pp. 17-21, illus.

New York, The Museum of Modern Art. *An International Survey of Recent Paintings and Sculpture*, May 18 - August 19, 1984. Kynaston M. McShine, Curator.

Gibson, Eric. "The Minimal and the Magical,"
The New Criterion, Vol. 3, No. 5 (January 1985),
pp. 42-44.

Krauss, Rosalind E., *The Originality of the Avant-
Garde and Other Modernist Myths*, Cambridge:
The M.I.T. Press, 1985, pp. 289-290, illus.

Yonkers, New York, The Hudson River Museum, *A
New Beginning: 1958 - 1978*. Essay by Mary
Delahoyd.

Gibson, Eric, "Thinking about the Seventies,"
The New Criterion, Vol. 3, No. 9 (May 1985),
pp. 45-48.

Stedelijk Museum Amsterdam, *Joel Shapiro*, 1985.
Essays by Marja Bloem and Karel Schampers.

Isozaki, Arata, "Joel Shapiro at Galerie Mukai,"
Yomiuri Shinbun (Tokyo), May 8, 1980.

New York, The Solomon R. Guggenheim Museum,
Transformations in Sculpture, November 22,
1985 - February 16, 1986. Essay by Diane
Waldman.

Ft. Lauderdale, The Ft. Lauderdale Museum of Art,
*An American Renaissance: Painting and
Sculpture since 1940*, January 12 - March 30,
1986. Edited by Sam Hunter, p. 85, illus.

Lodz, Archives of Contemporary Thought, *Process
und Konstruktion - 1985 in Munchen*, 1985.
Essay by Patterson Sims, pp. 214-215, illus.

Cooke, Lynn, "Joel Shapiro at Stedelijk Museum,"
Artscribe, June/July 1986, pp. 83-84, illus.

Los Angeles, The Museum of Contemporary Art,
The Barry Lowen Collection, June 16 - August
10, 1986. Essay by Christopher Knight, illus.

Merkel, Ursula, "Joel Shapiro," *Kunstforum*, #84
(June, July, August 1986) pp. 274-275, illus.

Madrid, Palacio de Velazques, *Between Geometry
and Gesture: American Sculpture 1965 - 1975*,
May 13 - July 20, 1986. Curated by Richard
Armstrong and Richard Marshall with the
Ministerio de Cultura, Madrid, Spain, pp. 118,
120, 125, 132, 140, 155, 160, 163, 164, 168, 174, 175,
179, illus.

Frankfurt, Frankfurter Kunstverein, Schirn
Kunsthalle Frankfurt, *Prospect 86*, September
9 - November 2, 1986. pp. 193, 194, illus.

Sarasota, Florida, The John and Mable Ringling
Museum of Art, *Joel Shapiro: Sculpture and
Drawings 1981 - 85*, October 31 - December 14,
1986. Essay by Mark Ormond.

New York, Janie C. Lee Master Drawings. *Master
Drawings 1859 - 1989*, October - November 1989,
pp. 56-57, illus.

Armstrong, Tom and Larsen, Susan C. *Art in Place:
Fifteen Years of Acquisitions*. New York:
Whitney Museum of American Art, 1989, pp. 175,
178, 185, illus.

New York, Whitney Museum of American Art.
The New Sculpture 1965 - 75, 1989. Essays by
Richard Armstrong, John G. Hanhardt, Robert
Pincus-Witten et al., illus.

1   Untitled, 1989
    Bronze
    70 x 80 x 30 inches
    (JS 866)
    Collection of the artist

2   Untitled, 1974
    Wood and wire
    3 x 20 x 10 inches
    (JS 920)
    Collection of the artist

3   Untitled, 1976-77
    Bronze
    4 $\frac{1}{2}$ x 10 $\frac{1}{8}$ x 5 $\frac{1}{2}$ inches
    (JS 155)
    Collection of The Modern Art Museum of
    Fort Worth, Museum Purchase with funds
    from the National Endowment for the Arts and
    The Benjamin J. Tillar Memorial Trust

4   Untitled, 1976-77
    Oil on bronze
    9 $\frac{3}{4}$ x 2 $\frac{5}{8}$ x 5 inches
    (JS 167A)
    Private Collection

5   Untitled, 1980-81
    Bronze
    11 $\frac{1}{2}$ x 17 $\frac{1}{2}$ x 10 $\frac{1}{8}$ inches
    (JS 391A)
    Private Collection

6   Untitled, 1979-82
    Bronze
    8 x 2 $\frac{3}{4}$ x 2 $\frac{1}{4}$ inches
    (JS 383A)
    Private Collection

7   Untitled, 1980-82
    Bronze
    23 $\frac{3}{4}$ x 13 x 8 $\frac{1}{8}$ inches
    (JS 465)
    Courtesy of Blum Helman Gallery, New York

8   Untitled, 1982
    Oil on wood
    12 $\frac{3}{8}$ x 43 $\frac{1}{4}$ x 13 $\frac{1}{4}$ inches
    (JS 466)
    Collection of Douglas S. Cramer, Los Angeles

9   Untitled, 1980-82
    Bronze
    25 $\frac{1}{2}$ x 21 $\frac{1}{4}$ x 18 $\frac{1}{4}$ inches
    (JS 467)
    Collection of Martin Bernstein

10 Untitled, 1982-83
    Bronze
    43 x 34 x 35 $\frac{3}{4}$ inches
    (JS 497)
    The Edward R. Broida Trust

11 Untitled, 1983-84
    Bronze
    30 x 11 $\frac{1}{2}$ x 8 $\frac{1}{2}$ inches
    (JS 584)
    Private Collection

12 Untitled, 1984
    Iron
    21 $\frac{1}{2}$ x 29 $\frac{1}{4}$ x 5 $\frac{3}{4}$ inches
    (JS 587)
    Collection of the Colby College Museum of
    Art; Museum Purchase from the Jere Abbott
    Acquisitions Fund

13 Untitled, 1982-84
    Bronze
    4 $\frac{1}{4}$ x 5 $\frac{1}{2}$ x 4
    (JS 593)
    Collection of Ivy Shapiro

14 Untitled, 1983-84
    Bronze
    80 x 79 x 39 inches
    (JS 595)
    Collection of The Saint Louis Art Museum,
    Gift of Mr. and Mrs. Barney A. Ebsworth

15   Untitled, 1985
      Bronze
      38 ¹/₂ x 28 ¹/₂ x 14 inches
      (JS 612)
      Collection of Loretta and Robert K. Lifton

16   Untitled, 1985
      Bronze
      90 ¹/₄ x 89 ³/₄ x 52 ¹/₂
      (JS 624)
      Collection of John and Mary Pappajohn,
      Des Moines

17   Untitled, 1985
      Bronze
      117 ¹/₂ x 132 x 72 inches
      Collection of the Baltimore Museum of Art;
      Ryda and Robert H. Levi Scuplture Garden
      Fund, 1987.3

18   Untitled, 1986
      Oil on wood
      54 x 12 x 10 inches
      (JS 712)
      Collection of Ernie and Lynn Mieger

19   Untitled, 1986
      Bronze on steel
      54 ³/₄ x 80 ¹/₄ x 42 ¹/₄ inches
      (JS 720)
      Collection of the Hirshhorn Museum and
      Sculpture Garden, Smithsonian Institution;
      Museum Purchase, 1987

20   Untitled, 1987
      Oil on wood and steel plate
      26 x 49 x 38 inches
      (JS 735)
      Collection of the Des Moines Art Center, Iowa;
      Purchased with funds from the Edmundson Art
      Foundation, Inc., 1987.8

21   Untitled, 1987
      Bronze
      48 ³/₈ x 51 x 34 ¹/₄ inches
      (JS 766)
      Private Collection

22   Untitled, 1987
      Bronze
      49 ¹/₂ x 15 ¹/₄ x 44 ¹/₄ inches
      (JS 767)
      Private Collection

23   Untitled, 1987-88
      Bronze
      135 ¹/₄ x 181 x 133 ¹/₂ inches
      (JS 790)
      Private Collection

24   Untitled, 1988
      Bronze
      72 ¹/₂ x 15 ¹/₂ x 10 inches
      (JS 793)
      The Edward R. Broida Trust

25   Untitled, 1989
      Wood and stainless steel
      119 x 28 x 24 inches
      (JS 865)
      Courtesy of Paula Cooper Gallery, New York

26   Untitled, 1989-90
      Bronze
      102 ¹/₂ x 43 x 78 inches high
      (JS 909)
      Courtesy of Paula Cooper Gallery, New York

List of Figures

Photography Credits

Geoffrey Clements: Plates 10-12, 21 and 25;
Figs. 1-4, 10, 12 and 14
D. James Dee: Plates 1-3, 5, 7, 13-19, 22 and 24;
Figs. 6 and 7
eeva-inkeri: Plate 8; Figs. 16 and 17
Susan Einstein: Fig. 13
Andrew Moore: Figs. 8 and 15
Wojtek Naczas: Plates 23 and 26
Douglas Rice: Cover
Ivan Dalla Tana: Plate 20
Jerry Thompson: Plate 4